THE ABANDONMENT NEUROSIS

The History of Psychoanalysis Series

Professor Brett Kahr and Professor Peter L. Rudnytsky (Series Editors)
Published and distributed by Karnac Books

Other titles in the Series

Her Hour Come Round at Last: A Garland for Nina Coltart
edited by Peter L. Rudnytsky and Gillian Preston

Rescuing Psychoanalysis from Freud and Other Essays in Re-Vision
by Peter L. Rudnytsky

Ferenczi and His World: Rekindling the Spirit of the Budapest School
edited by Judit Szekacs-Weisz and Tom Keve

Freud in Zion: Psychoanalysis and the Making of Modern Jewish Identity
by Eran J. Ronik

Ferenczi for Our Time: Theory and Practice
edited by Judit Szekacs-Weisz and Tom Keve

The Clinic and the Context: Historical Essays
by Elisabeth Young-Bruehl

Sandor Ferenczi–Ernest Jones: Letters 1911–1933
edited by Ferenc Eros, Judit Szekacs-Weisz, and Ken Robinson

The Milan Seminar: Clinical Aplications of Attachment Theory
by John Bowlby, edited by Marco Bacciagaluppi

*Ferenczi and Beyond: Exile of the Budapest School and Solidarity
in the Psychoanalytic Movement during the Nazi Years*
by Judit Mészáros

Looking through Freud's Photos
by Michael Molnar

Psychoanalytic Filiations: Mapping the Psychoanalytic Movement
by Ernst Falzeder

THE ABANDONMENT NEUROSIS

Germaine Guex

Translated by

Peter D. Douglas

KARNAC

First published in 2015 by
Karnac Books Ltd
118 Finchley Road, London NW3 5HT

© Presses Universitaires de France, *La névrose d'abandon* by Germaine Guex, in the «Bibliothèque de Psychoanalyse et de Psychologue Clinique» series, 1950.

Copyright © 2015 to Peter D. Douglas for this English edition.

British Library Cataloguing in Publication Data

A C.I.P. for this book is available from the British Library

ISBN 978 1 78220 191 5

Translation by Peter D. Douglas

Edited, designed and produced by The Studio Publishing Services Ltd
www.publishingservicesuk.co.uk
e-mail: studio@publishingservicesuk.co.uk

Printed in Great Britain by TJ International Ltd, Padstow, Cornwall

www.karnacbooks.com

CONTENTS

ACKNOWLEDGEMENTS   vii

ABOUT THE AUTHOR   ix

ABOUT THE TRANSLATOR   xi

TRANSLATOR'S PREFACE   xiii

SERIES EDITOR'S FOREWORD   xvii

INTRODUCTION   xxiii

CHAPTER ONE
Clinical description of symptomatology   1

CHAPTER TWO
Structures   39

CHAPTER THREE
Aetiology   69

CHAPTER FOUR
Therapy   81

NOTES   109

REFERENCES   115

INDEX   117

ACKNOWLEDGEMENTS

There are a number of people I would like to thank, and without whose help it would not have been possible to even start this project, let alone complete it. They are: Sue Graebner, the linguistic wizard who pored over every word of this manuscript and made many invaluable improvements, both to the work's technical sense and to its clarity; my great friend Terry Aspinall, who first gave me the belief to get up under the lights; Wilson Main, who never gave up on me; Margaret Hansford, who saved my life; the Gilberts, Viv, Dave, Geraldine, and David, my adopted family, who gave me that priceless sense of belonging; the 1972 38th intake of Marks and Morrow Divisions at HMAS *Leeuwin*—together we learnt to overcome and just what might be possible if you want it enough; and finally, I would like to offer my everlasting thanks to Dr Robin L. Chester.

For Nell, Jane, and abandonics the world over

ABOUT THE AUTHOR

Germaine Guex was born on 17 April 1904 in Arcachon, Aquitaine, France, and died on 20 November 1984 in Lausanne, Switzerland.

Her father, Georges Guex, was a native of Switzerland and a Protestant pastor. Her mother Hélène, née Millet, was French, and died when her daughter was still young. At seventeen, Germaine Guex moved to Switzerland and lived with her aunt. There, she studied education and psychology at the Institut Jean-Jacques Rousseau in Geneva until 1923, after which she worked as an assistant to Jean Piaget in the psychology laboratory of the Institute until 1930. During this time, she became familiar with the work of Freud, completed a training analysis with Raymond de Saussure, and became a member and training analyst at the Société Suisse de Psychoanalyse.

Above all, Guex was drawn to clinical work, so, in 1930, she was recruited by psychoanalyst Dr André Répond, director of psychiatry in the Malévoz clinic, Valais, Switzerland, to oversee a psychoanalytically inspired medical unit and psychological counselling centre for children and parents. Being both a therapeutic and preventative facility, it was the first of its kind, and became the model for similar institutions in Switzerland and France. Three years later, Guex contracted tuberculosis and had to forego this work. She moved to Lausanne, where she met her partner to be, the Swiss psychoanalyst Charles Odier (1886–1954).

After the Second World War, Guex began teaching at the Raymond de Saussure Swiss–French psychoanalytic education centre in Geneva. With Odier and Henry Flournoy, she sought to combine Freudian psychoanalysis with the genetic and psychological theories of Piaget. The research was, for the most part, inspired and shaped by their concept of what became known as abandonment neurosis, which they argued had a pre-oedipal aetiology, founded on the individual's fear of abandonment and need for affective security.

This research culminated with Guex's book, *La névrose d'abandon*, first published in 1950, which was, and still is, a ground-breaking work. Her research turns on two observations: the frequent occurrence of analysands whose neurotic symptoms are unrecognisable when measured against any of the Freudian diagnostic models, and the relatively large number of these patients who sought help from her, having already undergone thorough, classically Freudian treatments with analysts whose abilities and credentials were never in question, but who, none the less, could do nothing to relieve the suffering of these patients. What the analysands all had in common, Guex observed, were extreme, life-debilitating feelings of abandonment, insecurity, and lack of self-worth, originally ignited by severe pre-oedipal trauma.

Guex describes abandonment neurosis in terms of how to identify it diagnostically. She then goes on to outline every tool and treatment methodology, developed over many years of clinical practice, which can be deployed in the successful and lasting eradication of this pervasive pathology, repairing shattered lives in ways that seems to achieve the impossible, by helping these neurotics adapt to the rigours of reality and, ultimately, establish meaningful, ongoing relations with others.

Peter D. Douglas was born in Wembley, London, in 1956. In 1965, he migrated to South Australia with his parents on the £10 assisted passage scheme, and settled in the satellite city of Elizabeth. In 1972, he joined the Royal Australian Navy as a junior recruit and served five years, mainly overseas. He completed matriculation in 1976 and entered the Flinders University of South Australia the following year, emerging ten years later with a range of degrees and diplomas, including a Master of Arts.

In 1980, he began working as a performer, first as a musician in a touring band which also made records and actor into the late 1980s, then, into the 1990s, as a freelance writer, producer, and director of theatre, television, and film. In 1995, he joined Banksia Productions and began making television and film for audiences worldwide.

In 2002, he retired from commercial production and began lecturing in English at the University of Adelaide, and establishing the Bachelor of Media course. In 2006, he took up a position at Wilto Yerlo, the indigenous teaching arm of the University of Adelaide, mentoring Aboriginal students through their university courses.

I had been in analysis for about four years, and we were at an impasse. I knew what the problem was: the analysis had gone as far as it could and we needed to be working towards termination. The only problem was that I did not want to. The whole prospect had brought back the terrifying menace of abandonment, and my analyst knew it, too, so only ever broached the subject with the greatest delicacy, at which I would rail petulantly, then go silent for days, sometimes weeks, at a time.

During one such episode, a copy of Laplanche and Pontalis's *The Language of Psychoanalysis* fell into my possession and, as with all psychoanalytic texts that came my way during those times, I began devouring it. But on reaching page 270 or thereabouts, my interest suddenly blasted off the Richter scale. I had come across the entry on Germaine Guex and her seminal work, *La névrose d'abandon*.

From that moment on I was on the hunt for anything and everything Guex that might be able to reveal more about her theories on abandonment and the profound and long-lasting effects it had on sufferers. I brought it up with my analyst, of course, but not being at all familiar with Guex, he could neither confirm nor deny the validity of Guex's ideas, although he certainly re-affirmed that many of my problems did, without doubt, stem from issues of abandonment, as we had ruminated on time and time again.

Encouraged by this, and having scoured the globe, discovering the whereabouts of just two copies of *La névrose d'abandon*, I resolved to make an attempt to move towards termination of my analysis, the reason being, in part at least, because one copy of the book was located in the French National Library in Paris, and the other in the British Library, London; the time and effort involved in making a successful reconnaissance of either text could not be attempted within the working parameters of a full-scale psychoanalysis. So, it seemed that the positive prospect of such a venture outweighed all the abandonment fears prompted at the very idea of severing contact with my analyst.

Another discovery was that the book had never been translated into English. I resolved to make this my mission if I ever got hold of a copy, in which event I would need to re-hone my French. Someone had recently given me a copy of Albert Camus's *L'Étranger*, in French, which I had never actually read in French or English. I decided to translate it, and what immediately became evident to me, by way of an eerie coincidence, was that the character of Meursault made an iconic and prototypical case study, albeit fictional, in abandonment neurosis. Meursault's relationship to his mother seemed to have no affective substance whatsoever, and I found myself wondering if Camus was suggesting this emotional void was behind his protagonist's "autistic"-like disposition. I titled my translation *Intruder*, inspired largely by Camus's characterisation of the public prosecutor, whose courtroom rant paints a picture of Meursault, wrongly accused of cold-blooded murder, as an *intruder*, a clear and present contagion of danger evidenced by his moral bankruptcy and the fact that he did not cry at his mother's funeral, an intruder who must be eradicated as a means of preventing the spread of such virulence.

Close to a year went by while my analyst skilfully guided the analysis to its conclusion and I worked on *Intruder*. When the day finally came for my analyst and me to part, we said good-bye and I walked out of the door with a certain trepidation, but the sky did not fall in, which I took as an encouraging sign. I got straight on a plane to Paris and visited the French National Library. Unfortunately, I had an altercation with a librarian who took serious objection to the fact that I was not French. Consistent with the habit of a lifetime, I retaliated, foolishly perhaps, because, predictably, as was also the custom from time immemorial, I came away empty-handed.

I had a bit more luck at the British Library, and flew out of London a few days later with a photocopy safely packed into my carry-on luggage. On the flight back from Europe, I finished *Intruder*, and had intended to begin working on *The Abandonment Neurosis* there and then, but did not. In fact, when I arrived home, the manuscript went into the bottom drawer of my study desk, which is where it stayed for close to a year, never seeing the light of day. Why? I am not sure, but suspect that I feared the text might not hold all, or just some, of the answers I so hoped it would.

Then one day, a year or so on, I retrieved the first page, quickly followed by the second, the third, and so it continued. From then on, each page provided some form of revelation, however big or small, that took me personally on a journey of discovery, towards under-standing why I am the way I am, explaining not only that which was previously inexplicable, but exposing what for most of my life had seemed like the most horrendous of secrets. I interpreted and trans-lated each page as it came off the manuscript pile, never reading ahead. Such a temptation never occurred to me; each page was discov-ery enough as I worked through it, before eagerly moving on to the next, until there were no more.

Not surprisingly, then, for me, Guex's work is astonishing. Although, as I am quick to acknowledge, it might not have such a life-altering effect on everyone, it remains, none the less, a piece of trail-blazing research which unfortunately never seemed to receive the accolades or attention it deserved. Original publication did not get much beyond the French first edition, so Guex's ideas quickly fell from view, in addition to which the book was never translated into English until now, which I hope might just provide the spark and readership that will see justice done.

Peter D. Douglas, 2015

In addition to being always on the lookout for original works of schol-
arship, one of the aims of the History of Psychoanalysis series is to
make essential texts of the past newly available to contemporary readers. It would be difficult to find a book that fulfills this mandate better
than Germaine Guex's *The Abandonment Neurosis*. First published in
French in 1950, and translated into German in 1983, the present
edition by Peter D. Douglas at last brings this neglected classic to the
attention of the English-speaking world.

Douglas movingly describes how he came to undertake this project.
At an impasse in his lengthy analysis, and viscerally confronting his
own "terrifying menace of abandonment", he chanced in 2009 upon
Laplanche and Pontalis's *The Language of Psycho-Analysis* (1967), and
found himself drawn to their entry "Neurosis of abandonment", at
which point his interest "blasted off the Richter scale". So powerfully
did what he gleaned about Guex and her theories of abandonment
resonate with his own experience that, approximately a year later, he
terminated his analysis at least in part in order to be able to fly across
the world from his home in Australia to track down one of the extant
copies of the book in Paris or London. Having brought back a photocopy of *La névrose d'abandon* to Australia, it then took Douglas another

year before he could bring himself actually to begin reading Guex's monograph, but when he finally did so, "each page provided some form of revelation, however big or small, that took me personally on a journey of discovery, towards understanding why I am the way I am, explaining not only that which was previously inexplicable, but exposing what for most of my life had seemed like the most horrendous of secrets".

Habent sua fata libelli. Or, in the longer and more accurate version of the Latin phrase, *Pro captu lectoris habent sua fata libelli.* Not only do books have their own destinies, that is, but they have these destinies according to the reader's capacity to comprehend them. As Douglas's example shows, books, like an artfully conducted psychoanalysis, can have a transformative impact on their readers' lives. They can, indeed, become part of—or indistinguishable from—such a psychoanalysis, and clearly Peter Douglas was fated to be the translator of *The Abandonment Neurosis.*

As it happens, I myself had a second-hand encounter with Guex's work through the use made of it by Frantz Fanon in *Black Skin, White Masks* (1952). Among the eclectic array of sources on which Fanon draws in his masterpiece of psychoanalytically informed postcolonial theory, *La névrose d'abandon* occupies a prominent place, and so struck was I by the applicability of the extracts quoted by Fanon to my psychobiographical investigations into Philip Roth that I, in turn, quoted Guex via Fanon in characterising Roth as an "abandonment neurotic" and mapping the defensive stratagems to which he habitually resorts both in his life and in his art (see Rudnytsky, 2013).

Both Laplanche and Pontalis, as well as Fanon, of course, read Guex's book in French, and were steeped in the entire Francophone tradition of psychoanalysis, and there is an irony in the fact that only through the translations of their far better known writings has *The Abandonment Neurosis* heretofore made any kind of an impression on a handful of like-minded souls outside its linguistic orbit. But, as Douglas informs us in his biographical sketch, although Guex was born in France in 1904, she was of Swiss extraction on her father's side and, crucially, moved to Switzerland at the age of seventeen, where she resided until her death in 1984. Thus, despite writing in French, Guex herself remained untouched by any currents in French psychoanalysis, and indeed appears to have inhabited a veritable Galapagos

Island of the profession on which—apart from her clinical practice and her veneration of Freud—she was lastingly influenced only by the nine years she spent at the Institut Jean-Jacques Rousseau in Geneva, the first two as a student and the next seven, from 1923 to 1930, as the assistant to Jean Piaget in his psychology laboratory, and then, even more profoundly, by her collaboration with her life partner, Charles Odier, whom she met in Lausanne in 1933. Of particular note is Guex's connection with Piaget, which means she must also have known Sabina Spielrein, who was at the Institut Rousseau from 1920 to 1923 and was Piaget's analyst for part of that period. Although Guex does not mention Spielrein, Adrienne Harris (2015) has recently underscored Spielrein's importance in disseminating psychoanalytic ideas into cognitive and developmental psychology through her association first with Piaget in Geneva and subsequently with Vygotsky and Luria in Moscow, and Guex's integration of an allegiance to Piaget with her psychoanalytic orientation is exemplary of this syncretic tendency, as when she chastises Fenichel for making claims about "affective and instinctual reactions" in the infant that "leave aside the problem that surrounds the different stages of child intellectual development", and specifically because he refers to the ego in a way that "ignores all we know regarding the development of thought and judgement in the infant".

Despite Guex's remoteness from the ferment that was roiling psychoanalysis not only in France, but also in Great Britain and the United States during and after the Second World War, anyone who reads *The Abandonment Neurosis* today cannot but be impressed by her anticipation of, and convergence with, so much of what is now seen as foundational to both object relations and attachment theory. From the opening pages of the book, where Guex proposes that the "syndrome of anxiety attached to abandonment constitutes a neurosis in its own right", and that it arises at a "previous, much earlier, stage of the individual's development" than the Oedipus complex, and goes on to caution that the analyst who is "confined exclusively to the path of classic interpretation, although giving an impression that change is occurring, in reality is actually, more or less unconsciously, concealing the patient's neurosis", it is evident that her classification of abandonment neurosis as a pre-oedipal ailment parallels Balint's (1969) conceptualisation of the "basic fault", and that Guex's appreciation of the futility, and even harmfulness, of relying on "classic interpreta-tion" prefigures Winnicott's (1969) warning that when the analyst of a patient of this type fails to recognise the "central psychotic anxiety" and instead succumbs to "the patient's need to be psychoneurotic (as opposed to mad)", the analysis may become an interminable one in which "the patient knows that there has been no change in the under-lying (psychotic) state and that the analyst and patient have succeeded in colluding to bring about a failure", even though "the patient may even mobilize a psychoneurotic false self for the purpose of finishing and expressing gratitude" (p. 87). Guex's reference to "the infant's relationship with the frustrating object" is likewise evocative of Fairbairn, just as she foreshadows Kohut in attending to those cases in which "both an oedipal and an abandonment presence play simulta-neous roles in the structure of a neurosis" so that the analyst must be prepared to follow "these two causal strains, switching from one to the other depending on internal phases", while her overarching pre-occupation with the vicissitudes of abandonment constitutes an ex-tended meditation on what Bowlby would immediately recognise as a disorder of attachment.

If there is a weakness to Guex's argument, it lies in her minimising of the primacy of lived experience in the aetiology of abandonment neurosis, and a corresponding overestimation of constitutional fac-tors. Thus, she writes in her first endnote to the opening chapter that "the psychic repercussions are similar whether an individual has actu-ally been frustrated by the absence of parental attention, care, and love, or simply believes this to be the case", and by the term "aban-donics", therefore, she means those "who show symptoms of, but may not actually have experienced, abandonment". Later in the book, Guex goes so far as to assert, "Whereas with other neuroses, the emphasis must be placed on trauma that triggered initial conflict within the individual who is otherwise regarded as having a more or less normative orientation, in abandonment neurosis, the problematic crux almost always resides in a constitutional predisposition". In one of her clinical snippets, which is intended to call into question whether "the trauma from a real abandonment can ever be the essen-tial cause in the development of an abandonment neurosis", Guex tells of three children who "were living in the peaceful ambience that existed between their father and mother", when the mother "suddenly found great enthusiasm for another man, and no less abruptly left the matrimonial home". Whereas the two older daughters suffered only a normal amount of "chagrin", the youngest child, a boy, "sank into the shadow of abandonment anxiety", and did so, moreover, "having no previous history of the condition".

All this, in addition to being too sketchy to carry conviction, is unpersuasive on its face, since Guex overlooks the effect on the son of what we must imagine to have been the mother's dissatisfaction with her husband even before she ran off with someone else, and the idea that there was "a secure state that preceded the trauma" again does not look beneath the surface to the micro-abandonments inflicted above all on the youngest child due to the mother's emotional withdrawal, which are indeed experiences of "the absence of parental attention, care, and love" that deserve to be called traumatic no less than the obvious event of the mother's desertion of the home. Guex herself comes around to this conclusion when she acknowledges that "mostly we find that patients have a prehistory of the trauma", even though they may not be "consciously aware of the fact", because "their early life was often one of growing up amid a familial atmosphere that offered little security", but this crucial proviso remains unintegrated with her minimising of the impact of real experiences of abandonment and with her reliance on "constitutional predisposition" as the key explanatory variable in distinguishing normal from pathological outcomes. Even more jarring to twenty-first-century sensibilities is Guex's contention that "it is rare that an abandonic patient of whatever stage or type does not recount, if not a life of exclusive homosexuality, then one where it has been at least episodic", which reflects a heteronormative prejudice that was, alas, all too widely shared by psychoanalysts until the sea-change in recent decades.

But it would be invidious to dwell on any possible shortcomings of *The Abandonment Neurosis*. Even Guex's taxonomies, such as her contrast between the "positive-attractive" and the "negative-repulsive" abandonic, or her typology of "simple", "complex", and mixed" structures—however useful these may be—are not what is enduringly memorable about her book. It is, rather, her foregrounding of the existential anguish of abandonment—doubtless known to Guex from the early loss of her mother—which rests on the "tripod" of *anxiety, aggression,* and the *non-valued self,* that is sure to take the reader, as it did Peter Douglas, on a "journey of discovery" that is, like all the best psychoanalytic writing, also one of self-discovery.

Professor Peter L. Rudnytsky
Series Co-Editor
Gainesville, Florida

Introduction

Two clinical observations are the starting point of this work. First is the relatively frequent occurrence of analysands I have been fortunate enough to treat and observe in recent years whose psychic structure does not fit within standard Freudian descriptions of the neuroses, and who also demonstrate symptoms unrecognisable among any of the classical syndromes. The second, both a corollary and striking confirmation of the first, is that a number of these patients had already undergone lengthy and thorough classically Freudian treatments with qualified analysts whose probity and abilities are undoubted, but whose efforts did nothing to relieve the suffering of these subjects or their capacity to adjust to the real.

Both phenomena, it seemed to me, were important, certainly from a therapeutic point of view, so I decided to address them, in full knowledge of how difficult the task would be and the objections it would raise.

The first criticism of this work will, without doubt, focus on the way I apply the term neurosis to a conflict and disturbance of the ego, where the id plays a secondary or less decisive role and the superego, as Freud describes it, does not exist, because the individual never reached the developmental stage necessary for its formation.

Surprising claims perhaps, but the result of observation, none the less, and, as such, they are premises I will endeavour here to establish.

To retain the meaning of *neurosis* that we, as psychoanalysts, have endowed the word, I titled a previous work on the subject *Essay on the Anxiety of Abandonment*. In the time that has passed since, this phenomenon has been reinforced almost daily within the analytic setting, leading me to conclude that this syndrome of anxiety attached to abandonment constitutes a specific neurosis in its own right, because its symptomatology cannot be adequately aligned to any of the classical neuroses, and this is primarily because it occurred at a previous, much earlier, stage of the individual's development.

Freud concentrated his research on the relationship between biology and psychology. It is an account of our instinctual evolution developed from lived experience, and was seen by him as the producer of neurosis, which becomes the object of repression, as a result of intervention by the superego born of the Oedipus complex.

However, in pre-oedipal pathology, such as abandonment neurosis, we find ourselves confronted with an extremely active and fully conscious trauma that has been neither accepted and "digested" nor repressed. It is felt, and appears, as actual, in spite of its origins being so early and, in most cases, the sufferer's rumination is interminable. The patient creates the neurosis not because of unconscious eruptions, but as a continuum of self-provoked regressions and re-enactments, which results in the neurosis existing in two locales, infancy and the present: the subject constantly rebounds between the two, generating behaviour reflective of this confusion.

Thesis

The binding consternation central to the patient's mental life is problems of emotional security and a fear of abandonment, structured very differently from the classical range of neuroses described by Freud and his disciples. Here, we are faced with those still at a primitive stage of development, where all instinctual and emotional force is drained in one direction, driven by a single necessity: to attain the assurance of love and, consequently, the maintenance of security. From here arises the primacy of the maternal image, or the paternal image "maternalised", regardless of the subject's gender.

Under this circumstance, evolution linked to the emotional development of normative sexual instinct, with the establishment of an Oedipus complex as Freud described, cannot occur. However, a sporadic oedipal tendency can sometimes be detected, but it is feeble, always regressing to the infantile pre-oedipal, which explains the absence of a superego.

So, it is the conscious ego that opposes absolutely the admission of an Oedipus complex, a very primitive ego that cannot relinquish its objective, and renders inconceivable any admittance of the dreaded superego that would terminate the quest. Relations between the emotional and sexual, as Freud has stressed, are as subject to object. The two compete, or one seeks to conquer the other. This is a struggle that involves too much risk for the abandonment neurotic, which is why there is only ever the barest trace, or total absence, of an Oedipus complex. The one abandoned craves the sense of fusion with a single being, the mother, and can conceive of no other.

Classical analytic method applied to these patients, with slow exploration of the unconscious, does expose complexes we recognise: oedipal, castration, anal sadistic, oral, weaning, etc. All play an emotional role and must be interpreted as such. However, their revelation becomes increasingly ineffective for the abandonment neurotic. Moreover, not only is there an absence of patient amelioration, the analyst, confined exclusively to the path of classic interpretation, although giving an impression that change is occurring, in reality is actually, more or less unconsciously, concealing the patient's neurosis. Absolved by the very fact of their treatment and the analyst's lack of perspicacity, the patient's sense of abandonment in this kind of setting becomes reinforced.

Abandonment neurosis is the ego's domain, where careful analysis of experience, past and present, will eventually provide for the patient's liberation. This will be evidenced by a considerable development, a profound transformation with regard to consideration of others, themselves, and of the capacity to love, when, towards the end of analysis and often before seeking out an actual object, we see the patient make genuine oedipal advances: real signs of healing.

These, then, are the observations I detail in this work: evidence collected as a direct result of my clinical experience during recent years. Some will, perhaps, be struck by such revelations not being strictly in keeping with Freudian teachings. So I will emphasise here that I continue to hold that legacy, as it has been bequeathed to us, in the most revered esteem, as a revolutionary therapeutic method, an inexhaustible mine of observations and ideas, and an example of intellectual probity that was total.

In youth, we marvel at the genius of Freud's research and discoveries, but only through the advance of years and analytic experience, I believe, is it possible to truly grasp the vast scope of his opus, its massive impact, and the rarity of intellectual fidelity that was his. This rigour, maintained to the last, drove him to re-examine research outcomes over and again, constantly testing their veracity, even when it meant contradicting earlier assertions.

This, it seems to me, remains the most exemplary of precedents set by Freud: a continuous striving to apply the analytic method with an open mind, modestly contributing clarifications of how best to utilise this astonishing tool that he entrusted to us, along with an obligation to continue the work of studying and attempting to heal pathologies that he had neither time nor opportunity to address.

CHAPTER ONE

Clinical description of symptomatology

Generalities

A t the outset of treatment, if the therapist is not sure what to look for, the abandonment neurotic—whom, for convenience sake, we shall refer to from here on in as the abandonic[1]—presents nothing specific that might enable the analyst to make such a diagnosis. This is an important point that needs to be emphasised. First, because it explains why, until now, so many abandonics have been erroneously pigeonholed into classical neurotic disorders; and second, in an attempt to dispel the fearful fascination and subsequent abusive employ that greeted and has grown around the term *abandonment neurosis*. I am referring here to the fashionable popularity that abandonment theory seems to enjoy among newer analysts, which appears to stem from a number who, themselves analysed according to classical Freudian method, none the less remain fixed on that orthodox path, even when confronted with patients who demonstrate unresolved ego problems attached precisely to the anxiety of abandonment.

Abandonment neurosis is equally prevalent among men and women. We see adults aged, say, thirty to forty, as well as children and adolescents, coming to treatment. However, it seems the abandonic's disturbance—unlike in the other neuroses—has not appeared suddenly with an acute onset of symptoms. Rather, it presents as a chronic debilitation dating back to infancy, which, ever since, has noticeably disrupted character and behaviour and can quickly escalate to levels difficult or intolerable to bear through reignition of the original trauma from an external source and circumstance.

Initial contact and first impressions

The first contact between psychotherapist and abandonic is particularly delicate, for two reasons: first, because of a profound affective reverence the patient assumes towards the analyst, and second, through the diverse range of expression the patient employs to communicate the depth of these emotions. An initial objection here would be that the same can be said of all the neuroses. However, my experience has consistently been that an abandonic will, on initial entry into the analytic setting, demonstrate a more acute reaction, and furthermore, that *an accurate assessment* of this reaction is sufficient for us to avoid certain diagnostic errors.

The very fact of the abandonic's severe sense of insecurity and manic state, conscious or not, will place greater hope and expectation on the analyst than in the case of other neuroses. This hope and expectation—characteristic of the neurosis—is the expression of all primary need, made with the full imperative of the age to which it is attached. Our ultimate quest is to analyse this interior life, and the precise demands peculiar to the abandonic. Of interest in this regard is that the abandonic, from the very first session, casts the analyst in the role of crucial new object, able to crystallise all rapacity, as well as being a unique interpretative source, feeding the passive and aggressive affective states that necessarily arise.

One observation, both interesting and useful here, follows from the experiences of a number of analysts who note that the abandonic will usually play simultaneously on both passive and aggressive fronts, but whether there is a predominance of one or the other, it seems, is due, in part at least, to the analyst's gender. Generally, a female analyst, being less impersonal and technically driven than most male counterparts, comes to embody the original source of conflict: the mother, in which case the analysand tends towards the passive, the aggressive element having been repressed, not because of the intervention of a superego formed by an Oedipus complex, but from fear of it causing the link to be severed with the analyst-mother. A male analyst, on the other hand, more often tends to expose the patient's aggression. This is because the therapeutic setting can be less emotional—colder. The reason seems to be that a male presence has represented in the abandonic's life an ongoing source of consternation, although not, it should be emphasised, as a rival object. Interpretations of sadistic or masochistic transference in accordance with the analyst's gender are not hard and fast rules, but, rather, of greatest assistance when regarded as a general trend in the diagnosis and treatment of abandonment neurosis. By contrast, for the most part, the analyst's gender plays a far less dominant role in the treatment of post-oedipal neuroses.

So, proceeding in the face of hungry expectation from an anxiety-wrought abandonic, who also exhibits a full range of mechanisms that pull in the opposite direction, we resolve to dissipate the patient's anguish by analysing its structure and formation, not only to bring provisional calm but, moreover, to create from the very beginning—one human being to another—milestones of trust through the delicate, subtle role and weighty responsibility that the analyst must bear.

As mentioned, the second factor that significantly increases the problematic nature of our task is that the sheer diversity of primary data collected from the patient can be so vast. However, beneath this scope of diagnostic difficulty we can, it seems, roughly speaking, classify these patients into one of two main groups, depending on the degree of conscious awareness they possess of their own condition.

Patients more or less conscious of their affective condition

From the outset these patients recount with ease the frustrations, deceptions, and disappointments they were subjected to. They know their need for love goes unsatisfied because self-confidence is lacking. Characteristic also is the ongoing state of emotional insecurity and fluctuating levels of anxiety, all of which conspire to create a life beset with difficulty and ongoing struggle.

These analysands can be further separated into another two possible categories, but, before settling on one or the other, the analyst must make a thorough, unhurried examination of the patient's history, previous behaviour, and current difficulties. Only then will we be best able to determine whether the patient is either a genuine abandonment neurotic fixed at a pre-oedipal stage of development, or a more conventional post-oedipal neurotic, where the superego plays a role we recognise, but is combined with certain elements of abandonment that are secondary to the central neurosis.

Patients not conscious of their affective condition

These patients become preoccupied with peripheral problems in an attempt to steer the analyst's attention off course, which is an unconscious defence against analytic investigation and, above all, the dread of revealing a profound infantilism that is all but completely hidden from the self. It is worth noting that the abandonic gifted with greater intelligence, reasonably enough, has more chance of detecting flaws in an analyst's perspicacity. Often revealing vast gaps between certain elements of the ego and unconscious affectivity, these patients quickly reveal the truth regarding their actual degree of emotional development. An outwardly strong sense of security and self-value in certain fields tends towards illusion, masking a depreciation of these achievements as being of only partial and compensatory worth.

Furthermore, knowing themselves as adaptable and capable of success in certain domains, as well as being—by virtue of their neurosis—dedicated to, for example, moral, intellectual, and sometimes religious pursuits with absolute rigour, it is painfully difficult for patients of this type to acknowledge their shortcomings and failures and, as a consequence, come to accept that the love they so desperately crave is an infantile anachronism. It is from this vantage point that their ingenuity is employed to sabotage any meaningful analytic investigation.[2]

In short, whether a patient sets out to guide the analyst towards a diagnosis of abandonment neurosis or, conversely, away from it, we must exercise the greatest prudence before arriving at a definitive conclusion. So, care must be taken to avoid diagnosing the neurosis purely on the basis of identifying an abandonment and insecurity complex, for example, because there is every chance it could be connected to another disorder entirely: moral neurosis, notably. On the other hand, we need to be equally vigilant not to fall into the trap of allowing a patient to lead us away from an accurate diagnosis by missing, for instance, the core abandonment anxiety that is at the heart of this neurosis.

To summarise: upon initial consultation, nothing in particular seems to distinguish an abandonic from the other neurotic types. However, upon closer examination, we note that the patient's psychic structure is revealed to be fundamentally different in the case of abandonment neurosis. To avoid technical mistakes and diagnostic errors during the initial contact with patients, therefore, it is essential to clarify these structural differences, which alone can isolate the symptoms of abandonment neurosis, in an analytic setting that otherwise provides poor and often contradictory differentiation, and can potentially lead the analyst down a path of misinterpretation.

The problem of symptom classification

To my knowledge, no study exists that provides for us a thorough clinical description or precise definition of the psychic structures that formulate abandonment neurosis. With no illusions as to the difficulty of the task, I shall endeavour in the pages that follow to provide such a description, with particular regard to the ego, instinctual attitude, and what I call the bio-affective system of regulation, which is a necessary accompaniment. Any attempt here to align these elements with Freud's own description and definition of the ego, id, and superego, as has been emphasised, is erroneous, so, in the unique case of abandonment neurosis, we must first desist from classifying its symptoms around the dynamics of these three psychic structures as we would do routinely otherwise. Having tested numerous methods of classification, all of which were problematic, I shall confine myself here to an enumeration of the symptoms of the neurosis that is as clear and logically ordered as is possible. This is a procedure that may seem overly fastidious, but enjoys the advantage of eliminating the arbitrary.

Abandonment neurosis manifests as a series of varied emotional reactions that mark the character and behaviour of the subject from an early age, and that assert themselves with particular violence whenever a circumstance arises that provokes feelings of frustration and abandonment. Although these levels of intensity differ from one abandonic to another, all share two characteristics: anxiety and aggression, which is a regression to initial experience, characterised by an ego that lacks any feeling of value. So, we can say that the spectre of abandonment creates *anxiety*, which, in turn, spawns *aggression* and the *non-valued self*. This is the tripod upon which rests the entire symptomatology of this neurosis.

Anxiety

Every abandonment neurotic suffers anxiety, the intensity of which, depending on each individual case, varies greatly, ranging from a slight interior malaise to pure unabated anguish.[3] The condition is more or less chronic, aroused most often by the affective threats of frustration and separation, etc., which become reactivations of infantile trauma, sparking the crisis where love is absent and solitude looms.

This is to say that the abandonic will betray anxiety in connection with the role that other individuals of importance play in his or her personal life, so, when treatment commences, analytic scrutiny results in the patient being confronted with a renewed crystallisation of uncertainty and fear, as well as, simultaneously, a fulfilment of need and hope.

Example 1: Mrs X, married, a mother, who lives in terror of losing her family and finding herself alone. A friend of hers lost both parents just a few days apart. Mrs X, in the grip of a dark and intense anxiety, found slight relief by requiring her mother, father, and husband to be by her side day and night.

Example 2: Miss N, throughout childhood, felt her mother's rejection; she was a woman of little time and sentiment who greeted all expressions of affection with sarcasm. As a child, Miss N once brought a friend home, and, while witnessing her mother treat the little girl similarly, felt her own throat tighten, until she could not swallow. She began to tremble, broke into a cold sweat, and, finally, without explanation, stormed off in an affective eruption she could not control.

Example 3: Mr Z was materially pampered throughout childhood but totally neglected psychologically. He presented with intense anxiety and an apparent abandonment neurosis. His parents, staunch altruists, lavished attention on associates and strangers at the expense of their children. Now married, Mr Z cannot bear his wife meeting friends. Agreeing to attend a dinner party with her, on the evening in question, invariably an ill-tempered Mr Z, complaining of feeling unwell, returned home suffering insurmountable fatigue and anxiety. On good days he can cope until evening, but after dinner will ask to be excused and retire to bed, but when the anxiety is too intense, no words from his wife can induce him to remain: his pain having returned, he retires to bed, sulking like a child, clutching her to his side for extended periods.

Example 4: Mrs V, who usually speaks with ease, arrived at one session in the grip of an anxiety so fierce she was unable to utter a word; her anguished silence continued until finally Mrs V managed to say, "I heard you laugh." She then burst into tears and continued to sob inconsolably. Little by little, I learnt she had arrived early that day, and heard the session preceding hers conclude with laughter, which immediately revived memories from her past: "My mother would laugh with my older brothers and sisters, they were all much smarter than me and my mother preferred them. I was the littlest, a nuisance, and only good for telling off. So here it's the same, I bore you, I'm stupid . . . etc." Hence, feelings of inferiority and fear of being cast out, heightening despair and anxiety.

As every analyst knows, such cases are encountered so frequently further examples need not be cited. However, what concerns us most here, as I have said, is that they are subject to such a diverse range of interpretations, as listed below.

Example 1: some will detect in this patient the presence of an unconscious death wish, projected outward in her constant fear of losing close relatives.

Example 2: a tendency towards excessive identification.

Example 3: Mr Z experienced two and a half years of conventional treatment with a very good analyst, who concluded that the anxiety attacks I have described, as with other symptoms, were cathected in passive dependence to an older sister. This initial interpretation broke the attachment, liberating Mr Z, much to his relief, but it left untouched the crippling abandonment anxiety that continues to permeate every aspect of his life, relationships, and, in particular, his marriage.

Example 4: Mrs V's reaction went well beyond an expression of simple inferiority.

It is precisely the problem of interpreting the symptoms of abandonment neurosis that is the fragile focus of this work. We shall leave anxiety for the moment, but return to it in Chapter Four for a more detailed study in the context of therapy. The phenomenon of anxiety-related emotional insecurity and fear of abandonment has already been the subject of an extensive study by Odier (1956). So, in the pages to come, I shall continue to concentrate on the description of other abandonment neurosis symptoms.

Aggression

As with anxiety, abandonic forms of aggression are diverse and of wide-ranging intensity. Apparent or hidden, immediate or delayed, with levels expressed or restrained (for fear of rupturing the bond, perhaps), aggression is an essential component of the abandonment syndrome.

Here, we speak of a reactive aggression sparked by the privation of love in infancy, which may diminish, then disappear altogether, over the course of treatment. The distinction between reactive aggression and primitive constitutional aggression is, we know, signified by nothing definitive, it being sometimes very difficult to separate one from the other. Yet, this has been the key issue to resolve regarding the application of analytic treatment, which has been rendered inoperable in cases where such constitutional aggression dominates.

Because they are so broad in number and diversity, it is difficult to describe and enumerate all the different forms of aggression manifest in abandonment neurosis. It is, however, identifiable as being attached to most acts, thoughts, and feelings, except in circumstances where the abandonic has the complete affirmation of love. However, this truce brokered with anxiety is only ever temporary; consequently, aggression too soon re-emerges, because never far away is a rapacity so total, prompted by intense fear of losing the object, that any pretext suffices to claim the potential menace of frustration and loss. Under such circumstances, positions of attack are only ever relinquished in order to take up those of defence; the abandonic will never fully disarm, the danger is too great.

The clearest path for abandonics to channel aggression and satisfy rancour is to avenge the past by making others suffer as they themselves have suffered: the threats, frustrations, and, in turn, the abandonment, all become the direct expression of this need for revenge. Others are made to pay for the abandonic's sufferings, past and present, in thousands of subtle ways.

The insatiable need for love

The abandonic, by definition, knows nothing of altruistic love, but, rather, makes tyrannical demands for a limitless supply of love, forever citing as justification total deprivation of physical and emotional attachment throughout childhood. Thus frustrated, acutely so because of the inability to explain or accept that frustration, *the abandonic must have complete reparation*. Invariably, however, the balance sheet will always close in the red.

Example 5: An extract from the journal of a young analysand at the outset of treatment: "I have never forgiven my mother. For me the future must abound with love and pleasure that fills life's void. And all who love me, love me greatly, over and again, but can never love me enough to cure the deprivation of my childhood."

Just how, through the flow of life, this insatiable and often vindictive need for love is woven into daily experience is precisely what must be determined here.

Abandonic demand is compelled by a mentality that is fixed intellectually, morally, and affectively at the developmental stage in which the original traumas of frustration brought emotional growth to a halt. The remarkable work of Piaget on child thought and pseudo-morality has thrown much light on the specific laws that govern early psychic development. We shall see, when attempting to define the abandonic ego, what it shares with infantile mentality. Suffice to say for the moment that the abandonic, like the child, will revert to *magical thought* as a means of combating reality and thwarting the formation of internal affective relationships, with the result that security remains external and, therefore, constantly threatened. What is more, in this sense the abandonic, like the infant, assumes omnipotent rapport over all.

These few observations are sufficient to illustrate the gap between an abandonic's way of thinking and that which we call normal, so it is hardly surprising that the former's needs cannot be appeased by those of the latter. The two are separated by an incomprehensible divide, further exacerbated by a vast landscape of abandonic aggression.

Magical thought: if the abandonic claims a conscious and rational rejection of the supernatural, he or she will, none the less, behave as if the opposite is true. For example, the greatest proof of love an abandonic can claim from the object is not just to be understood, but that such knowledge be intuitively divined. Here, the outward expression of desire, or grief, is hidden by the subject in the covert hope that the loved being's omniscience will "know", and so meet the abandonic's need through demonstrations of interest and attachment. Alternatively, if the object is absent, the void is filled with self-reproach, anxiety, despair, and virulence at the stark proof of being unloved.

Magical thought finds one of its most frequent and varied expressions in certain manifestations of a mechanism that I commonly encounter in my patients and call "truth testing", which consists of the abandonic enacting a falsehood with the aim of its being contradicted by the object through, for example, exposing a false indifference in the subject, revealing a false choice, opposing a false rejection, etc., in order to test the object's gift of telepathic divination, and simultaneously provide assurances to the abandonic that he or she is worthy of involvement and understanding.

Example 6: Miss J, aged twenty, was heavily traumatised by feelings of worthlessness in the wake of her mother's complete indifference, compounded by the presence of a docile older sister, who, notwithstanding, was endowed with great intelligence. Miss J doubts all she is told and oscillates constantly between depression and revolt. Her life is entirely dominated by the need to know, and prove, the feelings she evokes in others. The office manager where she works, noting her fatigue, offered a leave of absence; she refused, in the hope that he would insist. She reciprocated the advances of a young man and they became acquaintances, but when he asked her out to the cinema, she declined for the same reason as her refusal of the holiday. Neither the office manager nor the young man knew the reason behind her blunt rejection. Deeply disappointed, the young man again approached and asked her to a dance, only to be met with an identical response. He subsequently decided to attend the function with another. Devastated,

Miss J devised a final scenario to put the "truth" beyond doubt. She approached the head of the night school they both attended and asked to be switched from the class she and the young man shared. Over the days that followed, she attended the rescheduled class beneath an intense emotional cloud, in anticipation that this time he would atone, worry, seek her out, and, ultimately, explain all in a great confession of love. Many times, invariably, her hopes and expectations were dashed. Miss J's entire life is a single sequence of such failures for the same or similar reasons. Incapable of comprehending that others cannot grasp her hidden motives, she observes with astonished rancour each repeat experience that confirms every appearance of her being unlovable. Subsequently, to dispense with any doubt that may arise or linger, the need for "proof" is augmented, and so the curtain goes up on a new cycle of this vicious drama.

Other manifestations of this "truth testing" mechanism, less reliant on the magical component, will most likely contain and reveal more direct forms of aggression. I am thinking here of the hardened, rigid resolve capable of generating either indifference or the abusive words and actions so often employed by the abandonic in opposing the object's efforts to dominate or appease. The displacement of aggression and the unconscious desire for vengeance, naturally enough, play their parts here, but the central motive for such behaviour is "truth testing" to see if, despite the subject's appalling behaviour, the object's love will hold firm. The measure of such endurance by the object under these circumstances is regarded as commensurate with love's strength.

The more aggressive abandonic type, battling an impoverished sense of worth, is analysed with great difficulty because of this mechanism. Usually, during the early stages of treatment, the analyst's authority is rarely tested, but when feelings of entrapment, threat, or separation intrude, and abusive words are communicated as actual aggression rather than inadvertent expressions of an intense need for understanding and security, or if, in other words, the subject loses patience, then the analysis is lost. If, on the other hand, this ordeal is withstood, then fruitful work can begin, and a strong positive transference will develop, built on the foundations of this all-new experience. The patient can then realise the dream by discovering his or her own magician, freeing the analyst to purge abandonic bitterness.

The abolition of intention: through the normal course of emotional relationships real sentiments, that is, feelings that govern subsequent actions, are considered to be of greater importance than the actions themselves, and may be subject to every sort of contingency. Such a disposition implies that a relationship is primarily a product of thought, the presence of which is valued internally, and that the individuals involved regard each other with feelings of reciprocity and trust.

If we consider this form of thought, and *intention*, beyond the bare facts, then also implied is the existence of a healthy interior security. All of this is lacking in the abandonic, who regards these and other words, such as "interior understanding" and "feeling", with caution as being deceptive. In their place is a quest for proof, *ad infinitum*, which consists precisely of exposing only the raw, brutal facts stripped of any context or circumstance connected with the object's intention. This is because, for the abandonic, anything peripheral to core need is not considered, not thought about, does not exist. What is sought are individuals who cherish reliability, exactitude, and certainty, or simply those who never, under any circumstance, fail to honour a commitment. The impediments, the causes of delay, the physical or psychological difficulties that can have an impact on the goodwill and desire of the object, do not exist for the abandonic, except perhaps in the most feeble of measures. Again, the hope is for magical proof of love: the object "could have" arrived on time if he or she "really wanted to", or "might have been" more talkative in spite of fatigue, or, in short, if there had been true desire, all obstacles would have been overcome. Here, a very primitive egocentricity, totally lacking in affective security, abolishes any sense of what might be possible, real, and contingent, and resorts instead to belief in the magical nature of the object's omnipotence.

Absolute need: the abandonic admits neither real contingency nor anything it may resemble. This pathological form of love is infinite, so only *absolute* satisfaction of such an avid appetite can provide a cure, or, at least, that is the affective experience recounted: no measurement, no limit, no restriction. In addition, there is a need to share all, to know all, and understand everything about the love object—which doubles as a protective measure against possible infidelity—while themselves wanting to be loved totally, absolutely, and forever. Abandonic attachment is monogamous, nothing is shared beyond it and absence is not admitted. If this pact is damaged, even slightly, it is destroyed, satisfying a commandment of "all or nothing".

It is not difficult to calculate the primacy of aggression's role in such an equation. Tyrannical in and of themselves, the abandonics' pursuit of absolute satisfaction gives rise to interminable demand, as dissatisfaction results in the creation and enacting of scenarios that are always cruel, sometimes sadistically so. The abandonic is also capable of externalising aggression through the deployment of passivity.

The passive position

Fixed at the receptive stage of infancy, the abandonic expects everything from others. In the more acute cases, not only is there an incapacity for reciprocal love,[4] but the subject is also fixed to a passive position within every area of life.

Example 7: Mr X is an intelligent and professionally active man, but is unable to replicate this competence in his private life. When clothes shopping, for example, his wife must accompany him. Interminable negotiations precede every purchase, as feeling between them quickly festers. Mr X projects his feelings of low self esteem on to his wife, convinced she judges him to be worthless, because she refuses to acknowledge his taste and needs.

Example 8: For Mr Y, when planning a journey, all pleasure evaporates as he is forced to begin preparations. Despite being self-critical on this point, he feels, none the less, a profound sense of injustice. He also demands that his wife organise everything on her own: passport, tickets, carriage, compartment, seat, and provisions for the journey, for only then, he feels, can he face the ordeal of separation.

Such mechanisms, naturally, reinforce inferiority, evoking a downward spiral of emotional strength: the failure to act reduces possible options, which further weakens the resolve to act. The abandonic is often overwhelmed by an inability to be active, which is, in fact, connected to an objective lack of experience, a poverty of recourses generated by passivity itself. But these shortcomings, often real, are also exploited by the abandonic in support of his or her neurosis, which serves both to prolong the security enjoyed by such a state of infantile irresponsibility, and to enslave others into the employ of satisfying the abandonic's needs. It is here we find the displacement of aggression tends to be inflicted on current objects, in retaliation for traumas committed by parents, with all the subsequent consequences. So, an inability to cope in isolation, which results from a lack of resourcefulness and the fear of responsibility, is also often seen by the abandonic as a direct consequence of never having been sufficiently loved. Here, in many instances, great satisfaction is drawn from the manifest exposure of proven parental guilt. If the parents are still living, vengeance will be exacted either directly through continued dependency on them, or indirectly by "shaming" them. If parental blame cannot be applied at the source, then the object is made to pay. Also, the relationship established between parental fault and the abandonic's inability to live reserves the subject's right, in his or her belief, to retain this passive position with all guilt having been absolved in advance.

Interpretations, fantasy, and masochistic behaviour

It may seem paradoxical here to consider expressions of masochism as being actual forms of aggression. I am not referring to the type of sadism Freud described, which is originally directed outward before being turned against the self, then repressed; rather, I am speaking here of the abandonic who demonstrates a masochism that does not fit within the Freudian framework. As Odier first noted (1956, pp. 272–274), it is necessary to distinguish between two types of masochism: the moral masochism that Freud described, and the affective, abandonic masochism. The later is primary, being partially constitutional, then exacerbated by the abandonment, so is not a product of superego repression. These mechanisms, developed and elaborated by the ego, are generally conscious or preconscious, and appear to play a double role: first to strengthen and justify the feeling of a non-valued self, which I will return to below, then second, and I stress this point, to feed the initial trauma so that it continually thrives.

Recognition of the distinction between the two types of masochism, moral and abandonic, remains problematic and warrants much closer examination. But, for the moment, it is important for us to note the primary role masochism plays within abandonic symptomatology, in addition to its sheer diversity, frequency, and the amounts of psychic energy it burns. Whether in the form of interpretation, fantasy, dreams, or behavioural disorder, affective masochism is one of the more striking characteristics of abandonment neurosis.

As we shall see, the structure of affective masochism is very complex and difficult to grasp. It is closely linked to the "truth testing" mechanism, so, accordingly, also relies on magical thought. However, the reason I stress the centrality of abandonic masochism here is precisely because of its aggressive qualities. In denying self-value, by lowering, degrading, and destroying it psychically, the subject knows only too well that the object can be engaged and, sometimes as a direct consequence, so, too, the culpable non-loving mother and father.

Three manifestly different types of masochism are identifiable within abandonment neurosis where, in particular, characteristics of the non-valued self and of aggression are inversely proportional and of varying intensity.

Masochism and truth testing: here, the subject naturally pays the price for putting others to the test by enacting the false attitudes, false choices, and false rejections, etc. that constantly deprive the abandonic from attaining what is desired, while reinforcing feelings of inferiority and states of dependence which, as we have seen, invariably end in desolation. This form of masochism is, for the most part, a secondary product of the malevolent "truth testing" mechanism, where the conscious desire for success is lost, trumped by the unconscious need to fail. None the less, the abandonic can, thanks to magical belief, remain a strong aspirant of happiness and love, despite being ignorant of the suffering it ultimately comes to cause.

Explosive masochism: by this I mean scenes of despair, which are crises of the non-valued self, directed against the object, where the onset of anxiety is more or less spectacular. Worthlessness, impotence, helplessness, and extreme violence are the *mêlée* of feelings churning within the subject that causes these affective eruptions. Here, although it may not always seem the case, it is aggression that dominates. To gain some consolation and reassurance, the subject might take the opportunity to disarm and punish the object by unleashing brutal accusations of guilt to crippling effect, because a function of these assaults is to prove that the subject is not responsible, while the object is held to be totally responsible.

Secret masochism: here, the abandonic's masochism exists in reverie and fantasy, with the emotional, rather than sexual, emphasis that accompanies all abandonment neurosis. Generally, these symptoms tend towards profound self-destructive urges, and are linked to feelings of worthlessness. Aggression, of course, also thrives under these conditions. During treatment, abandonics will recount malformed interpretations of reality to unreservedly exhibit a deep and fundamental distrust of themselves, others, and, first and foremost, the object. In fantasy, the object is capable of anything, the most appalling deception, infidelity, and abandonment. On hearing these stories, we cannot help but wonder what measure of positive feeling it might still be possible to arouse in the subject. The fact is, interior insecurity most often compels a nourishing of distrust, in order to avoid giving too much of the self, which, it is thought, will necessarily result in abandonment: if there is no attachment, there can be no love, no loss, no abandonment. The subject must be protected from the haunting expectation of solitude and abandonment at any cost, so fantasy becomes the risk avoidance strategy, which itself results in a shortcut to rancour and despair.

We have provided sufficient review of the principal components of abandonic behaviour to leave no doubt as to the fundamental importance of aggression among the symptoms of this neurosis. The analyst is sometimes surprised by the ingenuity and violence of its manifestations, but should remain mindful that however robust and tenacious this aggression, it has no purpose other than to signify an extreme need for security and love. Never underestimate the full emotional toll exacted on the sufferer, which is masked by these mechanisms of emotional defence or revolt, and the cycle where hope springs eternal, only to be endlessly dashed. Abandonics are most often individuals with very high emotional potential and a wealth of feelings which can be neither utilised nor dispersed beneficially because of emotional needs that were not satisfied during the crucial years of infancy and, as we have seen, it is always this initial privation that has given constitutional rise to abandonment anxiety and affective insecurity.

Confronted with this deprivation, the individual can react in either of two ways: if obsessed with the absent image, a bitter, vindictive, and aggressive support of suffering, accompanied by demands for appeasement, will be apparent. If, alternatively, the prevailing strategy is to acquire what is desired, then any means to derive satisfaction will be sought in an attempt to fill the void. Also contained within these two attitudes, and resulting from this lack of love in infancy, is *aggression*, at varying levels of strength: more intense when fuelled by the loss and subsequent damage that has been endured, less so when thoughts of gain, and possible satisfaction that may be won, are of principal concern. Furthermore, as we shall also see, the manifestation of either category does not just signify differing personalities; it also results from the sense of a non-valued self that is virtually total.

Two categories

Schematically, it seems to me possible, and practical, to distinguish these two categories of abandonic. The first is the subject who is inconsolably stricken by resentment for not having been loved, whom I call "negative-repulsive"; the second is the patient who, above all, must find love, whom I have named "positive-attractive".

Diagnosis always contains an element of the arbitrary, so care must be taken not to forcibly pigeonhole either category, which is why the following classifications are intended as guidelines only, and should in no way be regarded as rigorously definitive. The negative-repulsive, for example, also craves love, and is capable of devoted tenderness, provided approaches from others are made with reassurance. Equally, the positive-attractive is by no means exempt from rancour, particularly when menaced by abandonment, or simply frustration, when the result can be aggression and a need to lash out. I cannot say that either category is predominant, only that hatred on the one hand and love on the other represent the polarities, with every degree of variation in between.

Within the negative-repulsive, an obsession with the past, its frustrations, emptiness, and failures, has cast a paralysis over any life momentum. Generally more introverted than the positive-attractive, the negative-repulsive has a tendency to rummage through deceptions past and present in the development of a more or less secret thought zone, where bitter disillusion and resentments are harboured, which can look like a kind of autism. In contrast to actual autism, however, the abandonic is conscious of this secret zone, and cultivates its defence against all intrusion. More egocentric than the positive-attractive, the negative-repulsives keep very much to themselves and have very little capacity for reciprocal love, which is displaced by a retentive impulse towards aggression, and the constant need for vengeance. Inward withdrawal denies the negative-repulsive any positive experience that may compensate for the past. Add to this feelings of worthlessness and the consequent absence of affective security and the picture is almost complete. Being confronted by life and social interaction results in feelings of impotence, which leads to a total rejection of any sense of responsibility. Others are blamed for frustration and betrayal, yet amelioration is also continually expected of those others. Passive affective masochism, combined with the aggressive call to love, are behavioural characteristics. Others easily identify the negative-repulsive, but in a purely negative sense, which is to say indifferently, unless the subject is considered dangerous.

The positive-attractive abandonic, generally speaking, has greater ability adapting to the real. This category leans much more towards disquiet rather than rancour. So can he or she find love, be capable of maintaining that attachment and, ultimately, shift the spectre of solitude and abandonment? It is within the parameters of this question that problems can arise. The positive-attractive is active, striving energetically to fulfil these needs, though not without excessive disquiet, but nevertheless, in this way, often manages to obtain some significant relief from the neurosis by discharging large affective portions of it. In addition, if there is no risk without reassurance, and a guarded readiness to always withdraw if insecurity threatens, this abandonic is generally capable of engaging, at least partially, *vis-à-vis* whomever is loved. They do not suffer the same extreme feelings of worthlessness as the negative-repulsive. This is because they possess a greater self-awareness as to what is possible, along with some desperately needed feelings of value that permit a belief in attachment, while also providing a sense of interior security. Demonstrably sympathetic to others, the positive-attractive can identify, like the negative-repulsive, but inversely proportional, his or her own objectives which are aimed, through the use of others, at reparation in identical measure for past wrongs and full compensation for those injustices. This category of abandonic looks to others, and is capable of reciprocal love and devotion, so is able to find the security that is so indispensable.

This active empathy can, however, in certain subjects result in enslavement to others by projections of reparative need in the hope of gaining recognition and love. The mechanism turns from being advantageous to hazardous for the abandonic when pushed beyond a certain point. This threshold is the point of equilibrium between enslavement *to* others and *of* others. Having tipped the balance, the subject will often move from a position of empathy to tyranny and, accordingly, devotion becomes displaced as the predominant reparative strategy by vengeance.

Here, again, is an illustration of the importance, when dealing with psychological phenomena of such complexity, of maintaining a *relative* methodology to all demarcation and classification. It is imperative, then, to guard against any static conception of either abandonic category, as they have been distinguished here. These definitions, both convenient and practical, will prove useful as this exploration unfolds and will provide, I hope, greater rather than lesser understanding.

Non-valued self

So, anxiety and aggression generate obvious manifestations of the non-valued self, which, for the abandonic, constitutes a chronic psychic state, often adroitly camouflaged by a diverse range of behavioural over-compensation. At first, the uninitiated may observe that many abandonics seem to acquire a level of inner security and personal fulfilment but, as we have said, the ego is incomplete; certain elements can mature and advance beyond the mean, while others will remain feeble, infantile. Thus, it is possible for this kind of neurotic to enjoy genuine successes in certain domains, whereas in others, more closely aligned to emotional life, the sense of insecurity remains profound, rendering the abandonic impotent in the face of aspiration.

It is intentional that the term *non-valued* is preferred here to *de-valued*. Indeed, in the majority of cases, the original trauma depriving a child of affective security occurred during the early years, when all development still lay ahead. Consequently, feelings of self-value were also still to be acquired, so we are not referring here to a sense of value that has been reduced or lost, but, rather, one that was never gained.

The process by which a human becomes aware of itself as an object, as distinct from its surroundings, is now defined thanks to the work of psychological geneticists. Through direct child observation, supplemented by much research, we know the conditions and stage at which the infant discovers its own existence, and is able to distinguish the *me* from the *not me*. On the purely corporeal, or physical, plane, this distinction is relatively easy to grasp. Conversely, the psychic realm of thought and feeling operates in ways that are infinitely more subtle. The infant, driven by the instinctual laws of projection and participation, has a free rein in a much broader field, so easily confuses the me and the not me, precisely because of not constantly banging up against the outside world as it does when grappling with physical reality.

Even more baffling to us is the difficulty in calculating what is occurring in the infant when it becomes aware not just of its physical or psychical existence, but also of its value as an object. What is this concept of personal worth and how does the individual shift from an awareness of existence to one of value? What are the conditions and moments of this passage and, most importantly, what are the criteria that provide this sense of value for the infant? These are extremely complex questions that are difficult to address, given the current limits of our knowledge and, without making claims to answer any of them, I shall, none the less, in due course suggest how, in my opinion, we can tackle them profitably (see Chapter Three, p. 74).

For the moment, let us confine ourselves to an outline of five facts, as we know them, without additional comment.

- The first fact is that many individuals make no judgement on either the value of their personality as a whole, or of the individual elements that make it up. Their sense of value is flawed—there are gaps in so far that it is incomplete.
- Second, these gaps are concentrated in the affective domain. The individual doubts his or her capacity as an object to arouse sympathy and love in others.
- It is this sense of a non-valued self, unworthy of love, which is of grave concern and consequence, because it locks the individual into a profound state of insecurity that inhibits all relations with others, and, as a result, the subject's sense of worthlessness then readily facilitates an increasing depreciation of judgements brought to bear on the self.
- Affective non-valuation of self is observed only in those who suffered privations of empathy and love during infancy.
- Consequently, within all these individuals for whom the absence of love has been severely traumatic, an abandonment neurosis has been generated which has prevented and displaced the development of an emotionally valued self.

These facts allow us to establish the causal link in a subject who has suffered abandonment anxiety during childhood, with the subsequent impossibility of being considered worthy of love. As we know, abandonment anxiety in infancy is not solely responsible for the non-valued self, but it is an important contributor. We will return to this subject in Chapter Four.

The abandonic's sense of a non-valued self is expressed primarily in the form of unrelenting self-doubt, and can be voiced in the single phrase "I'm not worth loving!", which attacks anything that enters carrying the ability to form an emotional bond.

Example 9: Miss A, aged twenty-two, made a striking first impression, not only was she chic and outwardly charming, but also presented a certain distance, hidden beneath a hardened exterior. Obsessed by feelings of abandonment that circumstances of her childhood strongly justify, Miss A is not consciously aware of the feminine qualities she possesses; rather, her bitterness has led to the utter conviction that she is unable to attract others, is badly groomed, and has no taste; what is more, she believes herself unintelligent, which is far from the truth, and dares only to express such deeply held feelings to a rare few who are capable of creating a climate of reassurance and security. Her vision of self is entirely false. Professionally, it is the same; she cannot accept praise from superiors based on the quality of her work.

This case provides a clear demonstration of the strong abandonic tendency to judge the self and others from an exterior, rather than an interior, perspective by interpreting what is factually apparent in ways that fail to grasp real and profound meaning. We will return presently to this observation of abandonic *externalism* (Odier, 1956, pp. 14–17) applying the following corollary: absence of a capacity to internalise, profoundly and structurally, marks the particular ego specific to this neurosis.

The abandonic presents many tenacious expressions of self-doubt, which, when externalised, reveal their strength and force. These doubts tend to fix on to exterior manifestations of the personality or some physical blemish, around which all of the subject's insecurity crystallises: general manner, dress sense, deportment, a complexion too pale or too ruddy, bad teeth, skin, etc.; as we shall see, the significance of any imperfection is exaggerated by the neurosis as affirmation of self-doubt, but suffice to say for the moment it is a compelling

defence mechanism and character trait present in every area of abandonic life, manifesting in rejection of responsibility through the
subject's projection of internal disturbance on to the external.

Certain abandonics, however, possess greater consciousness of
their condition and are less inclined towards externalisation, recognising instead some of their interior flaws, which then feed feelings of
impotence: lack of intelligence, culture, artistry, intuition, sensitivity,
etc.; these deficiencies, whether illusory or real, are used by this abandonic to justify emotional disappointment and failure in the pursuit of
friendship or love.

The vast majority of patients—because this is exactly what constitutes their neurosis—are not consciously aware that the real cause
of their relationship failures resides in the type of love they seek
and, particularly, in the profound insecurity that governs their feelings
and actions towards others. There are some, however, who have a
greater recognition and come to the analyst full of self-reproach,
saying they do not know how to love, so suffer these consequences as
a result. Contrary to initial observation, this lucidity is not always the
province of those least afflicted by the neurosis, as evidenced by a
continued inability by these subjects to remedy their emotional problems despite their partial awareness, which usually denotes a tenacious masochism.

Abandonic self-doubt is reinforced by a mechanism that is also
rooted in non-valuation of self, where it is created in the equivalent
proportion—but positive rather than negative—and projected on to
others as over-valuation of self. This engenders a tendency to
constantly compare the self with those idealised others, to the subject's
detriment, as the vicious circle closes, having created one even worse.
These negative comparisons simultaneously reveal and reinforce the
non-valued self. The less belief there is in the self, the greater the
reasons that are found to doubt. In certain patients, these negative
comparisons can constitute a very real barrier to treatment that the
analyst must work to remove from the outset, if the analysand is to
concentrate on the self rather than the countless objects of negative
comparison that have been encountered between sessions.

Miss A, from Example 9, is a typical example of how violent this
obstacle can be. This young woman was so obsessed with the comparison mechanism that not once, during sessions covering a period of
more than three months, did she manage to fix on to any other

personal issue. It creates a level of agitation that goes far beyond the relatively simple resistance of conventional analysis, reaching a kind of compulsive externalism, that is to say, an incapacity to value the self independently of those others; it is a participation in an emotional milieu with a totally conformist ambience, the sole criterion of this environmental servitude is to bring down judgements that reveal the patient to herself in a necessarily unfavourable light. Only after three and a half months of treatment was Miss A able to generate an elementary ration of interior security strong enough to disengage her from the affective symbiosis of this external milieu, so that it became possible for us to focus on these problems without intervention being constantly necessary to actively deal with these obstacles of negative comparison.

The affectively non-valued self always leads the abandonic to obsessive and extremely painful feelings of *exclusion*, of being nowhere and everywhere at once, emotionally speaking. The primary and profound need for participation essential to all human beings is lacking in the abandonic, and has been from infancy, as is evident in this case of Miss A due to the absence of a strong emotional bond to either the mother or father whose love failed, along with, as a consequence, any integration into family life. From that time, she has remained generally alienated from all that is real in her affective surroundings, and believed this exclusion to be the work of others, when, in fact, it was self-inflicted through feelings of worthlessness driven by multiple fears. Distrust, aggression, and passivity were generated as a result, which, when combined with the non-valued self, formed a prohibitive barrier around her being, keeping the world at bay and the self protected. The abandonic feels excluded from that sense of security acquired during, and specific to, early infancy, so remains to greater or lesser extent a pariah, or, as one patient put it, *a love beggar*. Yet, this role of impoverishment, which, by implication, involves attracting the pity and charity of others, is greeted by some subjects with great repugnance, resulting in total isolation, a self-imposed solitary confinement which is both suffered and savoured simultaneously. This abandonic is silent—mute—on all that touches him or her intimately. This refusal to engage serves to maintain the initial exclusion. It is here that emotional masochism can exact a costly toll.

Even when not feeling excluded, the abandonic's ego is, none the less, still enfeebled as the result of infantile trauma, so cannot assume a normal position in affective relationships. This is because a feeling of being *insignificant* or *the other* is always retained and it is not difficult to conceive why these expressions, raised in the course of analysis, expose sentiments both bitter and depressive. Being *the other* is a description of self I have encountered many times in abandonic language. *The other* is someone preferred as absent, not needed at all, surplus to requirement. Being *the other* is a continuous sense of instability, ever on the look-out for expected repudiation, abandonment, etc., always working unconsciously to ensure the prophetic catastrophe is self-fulfilling. This is the sole emotional drama to which many abandonics feel they must aspire, always claiming to be the one singled out for derision, the Cinderella substitute. *The other* conveniently explains their lack of confidence and the absence of a valued emotional self.

Being *the other*, or, worse still, null and void with no place or part to play, is to feel horrifyingly alone and totally powerless to alter that circumstance. It is difficult to grasp the appalling depth of suffering that accompanies this state of abandonment, which, on the one hand, is attached to primal experiences of exclusion during infancy revived with identical acuity in adulthood and, on the other, contradicts the primary and fundamental human requirement rooted in the need to be included, integrated as a part of the whole.

The following is an extract written by a patient who came to analysis suffering an abandonment crisis:

> "The profound pain of solitude will, perhaps, always be suffered when there is an absence of harmonious fusion from that which is exterior to us. This fusion can be achieved either in the love of another person or, on a higher level, in the love of God. Harmony with the world is created in our absorption by it, and of it, isolation thus dissipates; it is the search for this solution that torments us so intensely.[5]

This feeling of exclusion, or being *the other*, poses a problem of interpretation for us as analysts, primarily because its triangular form resembles a re-living of the Oedipus complex, where we commonly identify superego sanction. In the case of abandonment neurosis, however, this "triangle" assumes a very different form, which will be demonstrated in Chapter Four.

We shall now consider an expansive and important area that is also closely linked to the non-valued self: fear, broad ranging and intense enough to paralyse the abandonic. It comes under the spectre of dread and anxiety that threatens the infant from dangers existing in the external world, which is made up of formidable beings and objects, the vast measure of which equals parental failure to create the environmental climate of security that is so essential. With no sense of an emotionally valued self, the enfeebled infant is powerless to combat such terrors. The adult that the infant becomes then inherits the affliction: it is a life where the self has been formed prematurely, with no sense of worth, so is incapable of adapting to what remains a hostile and inaccessible reality.

Whether or not suffering the effects of anxiety, the abandonic is more or less constantly menaced by a *sense of impending catastrophe*, which can intrude on any physical or psychological plane, so maintaining a constant state of tension and alarm. The misfortunes of childhood, followed inevitably by those that flow from the neurosis, become inexorable fatalities, a destiny that seems forever fixed.[6] Thoroughly schooled in misery, the abandonic easily recognises representations of happiness and is also able to create belief and resolve enough in advance to pursue it. However, these rigours can demand considerable effort, often over and above what is possible. Ultimately, catastrophe is the abandonic's outlook, so, if some happy and reassuring circumstance should happen to alter this ambience, even slightly, it prompts a reawakening of primitive insecurity, reinstating belief in the ill-fated destiny.

In breaking with classical interpretations of these phenomena, Odier has demonstrated that abandonic anxiety and fear, whether from the waking or sleeping hours (nightmares), possess all the characteristics of primary terrors caused by those same omnipotent and evil objects that confront the infant. Thus, we have observed that adult abandonics fix on anxieties and fears that are rooted in infantile terror, but each with their own particular idiosyncrasies.

The abandonic's fears are in the cosmic, physical, and psychological realms. Without claiming the list is complete, because any object can be coated with destructive magical powers and anything can participate symbolically in the primary terrors of infancy, I have included here only those most frequently observed.

Cosmic fears

- Fear of earthquake.
- Fear of being swallowed as the earth gapes.
- Fear that the earth will stop rotating and plunge from orbit.

Physical fears

Danger
- Fire, water, electricity, electric storms.
- Cavernous, steep slopes.
- Trains, cars passing outside.[7]
- Weapons, blunt objects.
- Wild animals, particularly male (e.g., bulls).
- Symbolic animals—mice, spiders, etc.

Disease
- Venereal.
- Cancer.
- Skin complaints—fear of becoming an object of repulsion.

Death
- Death is a twofold problem for the abandonic that we shall study presently.

Psychological fears

- The centrepiece is fear of love's absence, or its loss.

Fear of revealing the true self

This is a vast and diverse area. It includes fear of deception, displeasure, annoyance, boredom, etc., and, as a consequence, a belief in the impossibility of forming a sympathetic bond with another or, if one should develop, a conviction that it will not survive. The abandonic doubts his or her capacity to be loved, precisely because of the cruel blow of abandonment life has dealt, so will make genuine, but very subtle, appeals to the humanity and kindness of others. There is some truth in this belief that the abandonic cannot attract love, so it is easy to understand the need for camouflage or, conversely, the abandonic attempts to be all things to all people and never to reveal the true self. These fears are not only subjective, they have an objective basis also, in that abandonics' suffering is difficult for others to grasp or understand, because so little is known of their psychological plight. In addition, their suspicious, demanding, contrary, anxious, and aggressive character traits tend to repel rather than attract or be conducive to attachment. Abandonics know or can foresee this, so prudently disguise their innermost being. However, sitting alongside this relatively rational reticence to reveal themselves as they are is the subjective, totally unjust burden of fear they experience due solely to feelings of worthlessness. Generally, the abandonic knows too little of what, in his or her true being, will evoke judgements of merit, esteem, and sympathy, or simply value, in the eyes of others; thus, there is a dread of surprise intimacy because of the belief that there is nothing good to reveal or be surprised by. Rather, the strategy becomes to evade and conceal.

Attached to this fear of revealing the true self are communicative phobias such as fear of using the telephone, and of written correspondence. "I cannot speak to anyone without seeing their face."

One analysand told me, "I'm scared of saying something that will offend them without me either knowing or seeing the need for reparation."

Not to immediately know or see the reaction of another creates anxiety. Here, the subject cannot be reassured, because there is no means of knowing if the bond with the other remains intact or is being distended, so the fear is constant.

Miss A, from Example 9, was incapable, at the beginning of her analysis, of engaging in written correspondence with anyone but her parents, to whom she occasionally addressed some lines, being careful to keep their composition as banal as possible. She took considerable time summoning the courage to send them a few postcards, written as little self-indictments that would be proofread, and reread before posting: no need to more than mention here the significance of any reply that was even slightly delayed. After receiving some encouragement from this side, emboldened, Miss A wrote me some letters, personally delivered, but on this occasion truly intimate. I took care to read them in her company, demonstrating that the possibility of discussion arising apropos a letter can be a valuable primary means of expression, just as with conversation, which served to dismantle her belief in written thought as black magic. Next, she was able to send them via the post, then wrote to others, and was amazed when the replies did not identify her as a source of annoyance—in fact, quite the contrary.

Fear of emotional risk

The anxiety of abandonment and the dread of solitude generate in the abandonic an intense fear of anything that may risk their onset. In the realm of human relations, the abandonic is tormented by this risk, which is seen everywhere and has to be constantly guarded against. Impulses are inhibited through fear of possible deception. Sensitised by failure and extremely vulnerable to misunderstandings synonymous with lack of love, the abandonic suffers at a level objectively disproportionate, obsessed by the risk of deception and affective pain, to the point of not daring to live as such. This is particularly true of the negative-repulsive and is shared, but to a lesser extent, by the positive-attractive.

Fear of responsibility

To avoid this risk, the abandonic either engages with no one emotionally—the negative-repulsive—or on a level where serious risk is reduced—the positive-attractive. In general, both abandonic types dread responsibility and project it on to others. Not only are the past tragedies of childhood and the failures that have followed *the fault of others*, but, in present affective relationships also, if an incident arises the abandonic will assume complete exoneration. The reasoning is as follows: "My reaction would have been different if I'd been treated fairly." This way of thinking and feeling is very close to the "Well, they started it" encountered in children. In this regard, the abandonic is a prisoner locked in a vicious circle: fears and feelings of impotence generate a disposition of irresponsibility, which, in turn, nourishes those fears and that impotence.[8]

We could enumerate many other abandonic fears, but each would be attached to one of the three categories cited: fear of revealing the true self, fear of affective risk, and fear of responsibility. These three fear groupings have their origin in the initial anxiety generated in the face of solitude and abandonment.

It seems unnecessary here to provide more detail and examples. By contrast, however, what cannot be over-emphasised is the unexpected role that fear plays, and the infinitely expansive range that it has within abandonment neurosis. The threat of conflict, rupture, separation, isolation, solitude, lack of love are the latent terrors of every abandonic. Dependent upon the goodwill and charity of others, they live in a state of chronic fear.

False sense of self

Rendered affectively worthless as a result of the anxiety generated throughout infancy and childhood, with these feelings subsequently and constantly reinforced in the adult by the mistakes and failures of a chaotic life, the abandonic is endlessly dogged by a generally vague and incoherent false sense of self. Like all who suffer feelings of inferiority, the abandonic oscillates between excessive self-doubt and ambition. Unable to grasp the concept of moderation, everything in life becomes exaggerated, leaning sometimes towards excess and sometimes towards abstinence. Inevitably, these fantasies run up against the sanction of reality, and the stark comparison between what *could be* and what *is* reignites despair.

Generally speaking, the abandonic possesses two images of self that are more or less clear: an image of what he or she could have become subject to a presence of love and reassurance, and the distorted and negative image that the individual believes he or she has, in fact, become. Every abandonic conserves these two images, but which takes precedence over the other depends on the subject. It is useful here again to distinguish between the two categories of abandonic.

For the positive-attractive, the travesties of infancy and childhood are more or less reparable. If lack of love arrested childhood development, thereby also afflicting the adult personality, the positive-attractive knows, none the less, that certain potential opportunities have been retained and believes that reparation of the past is possible, if the present can provide the necessary love and security. The positive-attractive is supported in this belief by the evidence of an active life, which the fear of risk is unable to quash completely. This relatively vibrant life provides opportunities to weigh up the chances of success, to measure real possibilities, which sometimes allows positive-attractive abandonics to make favourable comparisons of themselves with others.

So, we can say that the positive-attractive possesses a relatively objective sense of self that is not totally without value, thus it is positive, while, at the same time, it is also a sense of self that remains affectively incomplete. What must be emphasised here, however, is that positive-attractive judgement is unstable and changes. It varies following fluctuations in security that are affected by the real, so that the self can sink in a moment of profound depreciation if love and security are undermined. These oscillations make the positive-attractive more sensitised than the negative-repulsive, who would never aspire to such elevated levels of self-value.

The negative-repulsive is felt to be the irredeemable victim of a past that can be neither forgiven nor forgotten. Part of the rancour is born of the belief in what could have been possible, if only the due ration of love and understanding had been received. Always accompanying this sentiment is the conviction, to a greater or lesser degree, that the injury is irreparable and that, as a result of the ill-fated injustice of others, all potential has been virtually destroyed.

"The heart can forgive, the injured psyche cannot", noted one analysand of this type. It is a partially justified remark, but an exaggeration, which corresponds to the sceptical and pessimistic mentality that characterises this category of neurotic. A prisoner confined within the self, the negative-repulsive feeds irreparable sentiment through continual loss, or lack due to passivity. No positive experience can rectify this idea of self because its position is fixed and can barely evolve, in the affective realm at least. Also, with the exception of some privileged domains, intellect and profession, for example, a fundamental sense of worthlessness is always conserved.

We can conclude that the affectively non-valued self systematically devalues all that creates personal inner wealth and inevitably leads the abandonic, of whatever type, into a distorted, false idea of self, in the sense of self-depreciation, even if the subject assumes an adult persona and has no conscious awareness of their infantile emotional state.

It is essential to stress that here the ego's injury is much more severe than the feelings of superego guilt and inferiority born of the Oedipus complex. To feel guilty is still to exist and live, whereas to feel worthless so often results in a "non-existence", maintained and reinforced by affective masochism.

Lack of self-respect and any real interest in the self

This symptom flows automatically from the precedents outlined above. It does, however, require some additional comments. The absence of self-respect is observed in every abandonic, subject to the differences and variations of self that we have noted. Lack of self-respect has, in effect, as many nuances as there are degrees of self-depreciation and its manifestations are diverse, sometimes seen as purely physical and external—poor personal hygiene or neglected appearance, for example—and sometimes experienced solely on a psychological level. When overestimating others in a measure equal with self underestimation, the abandonic applies the rule "two different 'weights' makes for two different 'measurements'" to his or her detriment, which demonstrates how the abandonic uses criteria to assess others that are not applied to the self, so value that may be due is not credited. In other words, there is a negation of reciprocity that is biased in favour of others, as was emphasised in *The Insatiable Need for Love* (see Chapter One, p. 9), but, in that instance, with the abandonic as beneficiary. The two observations might appear contradictory, but are, in fact, complementary: the abandonic who needs to attract others may very well be the same one who, elsewhere, has no self-value or self-respect, so here different behaviour is adapted to different circumstance. In terms of the neurosis and its emotional toll, other individuals are not considered; the subject is central and makes continuous demand for reparation. The moral, social, and intellectual domains, on the other hand, are considered by the subject to be of such—overestimated—value that the abandonic feels unworthy of being treated and judged against such lofty standards.

This lack of self-respect results from a simultaneous cause and effect, stemming from the inability to form an objective opinion on the diverse elements that make up the subject's own personality. From there develops an absence of interest in the personality proper, its capacities, talents, and tastes. Many abandonics live ill-conceived lives. With just themselves for company and no support, they go alone to the theatre or cinema and neglect to cultivate intellectual life or artistry, regardless of the desire to do so. For them only one thing counts: attachment to the object or, in its absence, fear of love. Emotional life does not really stretch beyond this, so that anything elsewhere that could enrich life is not considered. They lack true love of self.

Example 10: Mrs E, outwardly affecting an attitude of self assurance, lives in a state of acute emotional insecurity. Her contrasting behaviour on these levels, emotional intimidation on the one hand, combined with a broad ranging social life on the other, is typical and striking. Regarding her husband, Mrs E is always, more or less, hostile. She claims he is selfish, ignores her and the duties required of him. However, unconsciously, it is actually she who neglects him, by refusing to prepare food, tend to his clothing, or approve of his weekly *soirées* with fellow returned service veterans. Week in and week out, she reproaches him and takes her revenge by lavishing meticulous attention on others. She not only treats her young maid with much greater consideration, but also suffers pangs of conscience when spending time in the garden with a book, or at the piano, which requires the maid to be solely and fastidiously occupied with her work. If the weather is inclement, Mrs E will do any shopping herself, so not to expose her maid,[9] or any errand boys, to the rain. Invited to a friend's house, Mrs E was hesitant to accept, oblivious that others might enjoy her company; on the contrary, she was paralysed by the belief that she has nothing to offer and her presence would prove vexatious to all. She dares not devote time to her piano, despite plenty of opportunity and the pleasure it provides, in the wake of the judgement: "It cannot relieve the pain", etc.

A denial of interest in that which provides pleasure and fulfilment to the self is particularly striking in the positive-attractive, for whom anything not concerned with conquering the love object is *disaffected*. Alternatively, as we have seen, the negative-repulsive will apply the protective idiosyncrasy of refusing to engage with anything exterior, and push towards cultivating an isolated inner self by becoming obsessed with a number of these likes, personal interests, and habits. If, judged superficially, these two reactions are seen as different, they do undoubtedly share the lack of self-worth and the lack of self-respect.

Self-destructive masochism

We cannot close this section on abandonic manifestations of the non-valued self without again broaching the topic of masochism. I previously described this important mechanism as an expression of aggression,[10] in particular what I called explosive masochism, which are manifestations more destructive to the object than the subject. By contrast, we have seen, in the case of secretive masochism experienced in fantasy and dreams, where the masochistic component wins out over aggression, so, as such, has its place here, simultaneously extending and reinforcing abandonic sentiments of the non-valued self.

To summarise, we have demonstrated that the component parts of anxiety, aggression, and the non-valued self form the foundations of all abandonic symptomatology. Separately, or, more often, combined, they determine the totality of abandonic psychic life and behaviour, and I have attempted to provide here direct examples of what analysts can expect to observe on a daily basis within the clinical setting.

Also worth mentioning again is that among the abandonic's neurotic symptoms are a series of typical reactions, protective measures, which defend against anxiety, and, in a field very close by, are two juxtaposing attitudes that will be explored in due course, and that are adopted by the abandonic faced by an inescapable fact that is of singular importance: death.

Protective measures against abandonment

Haunted by the fear of losing love, the abandonic seeks to retain the tragedy, especially the anxiety that accompanies it, through the use of protective measures, sometimes positive, sometimes negative.

Among the positive protective measures are devotion and enslavement to others, where care is taken to preserve the bond by avoiding disagreement and opposition, by affirmation of the self, and by repression of all negative sentiment. The fear of losing love can result in all aggression becoming totally repressed and a subsequent inability to produce any conscious feelings of hatred. Through these mechanisms of attachment, the abandonic seeks to conserve and maintain possession of the object, whatever the cost.

Negative protective measures, by contrast, are focused on a refusal to attach, resulting in disengagement with any such development or sentiment because it is viewed as impending catastrophe. Negative protective measures include refusal to engage the self, rejection of responsibility in affective relations, a tightening of defence against emergent feelings of trust towards others and, consequently, a shrinking from the risk of love. Premature disengagements such as *leaving before being left* and *destroying before losing*, etc., are essentially driven by abandonic anxiety: initially to consume the threat, because the expectation of it becomes intolerable, and, second, to create a sense of power and satisfy the need for revenge. So, seizing the initiative, the abandonic turns abandoner, thereby avoiding a repeat experience of falling victim and being at another's mercy.

Example 11: Miss I, aged twenty-three, made a good start to her analysis, initiating a strong positive transference, and presented as a young woman demonstrating classic symptoms of an abandonment neurosis. Her infancy and childhood were lived in the menacing grip of a sadistic grandmother, which was consistent with her profound affective insecurity. After five weeks of treatment, a skiing accident temporarily interrupted the analysis. Upon resuming, a deep sense of sorrow was immediately apparent in Miss I. Then, as each day passed, she became even more sombre and increasingly hostile, not only to her immediate family, but also, especially, in the words she directed at me. The more time passed, the more Miss I, now completely resistant, ranted against analysis and analyst, to the point of fever pitch, finally demanding that I destroy all that had been healed in her, as the family had warned. Knowing her history, I presumed that an extremely violent crisis of abandonment anxiety had triggered a mechanism that said: "destroy, so not to lose". Then, effectively half way through a subsequent session, having arrived very tense and hostile, she broke down in a flood of tears, begging that I not abandon her.

Do not be tempted to retaliate against this type of patient by returning their aggression. It is obvious that there exists in this subject a constitutional element playing a fundamental role, manifest through rigid paranoia bubbling up and a primal hostility verging on levels of the grandmother's sadism, as both an expression of it and a reaction against it. However, positive results from subsequent treatment confirmed that the neurosis was strongly aggravated by the agitation of this constitutional element, verifying a diagnosis of abandonment neurosis. It became evident that the patient had often protected herself against the anxiety by the kind of desperate defensive action that the accidental interruption to treatment had permitted me to observe.

It is not unusual to encounter, towards the end of an analysis, whether in the case of abandonment neurosis or other pathologies that contain abandonic components, sudden manifestations of hostility aimed at the analyst: criticism, demands, a need to find the analyst at fault . . . etc. Here again, as I have indicated, a question of interpretation is posed. On numerous occasions, I have seen such manifestations linked to a real sense of development in the patient towards emancipation, affirmation of the self, and autonomy. However, it is by no means always the case. If, in some instances, the patient has precise knowledge that allows us to specify, this interpretation is justified. Otherwise, it seems to me, these manifestations are generally due to anxiety generated by the approaching termination of analysis, which, felt as an impending abandonment, is the expression of intense need for a defence against premature detachment, in addition to being another sign of an enfeebled ego.

The abandonic and death

Of all human kind, it is easy to understand why the abandonic has the greatest difficulty being indifferent to the problem of death. The abandonic, who cannot disentangle separation from anxiety, who is obsessed with loss of the cherished being, and who aspires to total and eternal possession of love, cannot fail to see death juxtaposed as either the greatest terror or the ultimate deliverance. These are observations that have been confirmed over and again.

Without assigning one or the other of these positions to a defined abandonic category, it is evident that certain subjects crystallise their magical thought and multiple fears around the idea of death, while others, in contrast, convinced that life will deny them, pin all hope on it, seeing death as a form of absolution. Experience leads me to believe that it is the latter, those who welcome death, who are the most frequently occurring. Odier was the first to confirm these findings in relation to dreams and or fantasies of the double death (1956, pp. 266–268).

Along with the abandonic, it is not difficult for those who enjoy psychological health to conceive of anxiety, terror, death, the inexorable limits of life, the ultimate separation from loved ones, destruction, and non-being. However, what differentiates the abandonic is the haunting obsession with taking the idea of death, as well as the anxiety it triggers, and unconsciously linking it to separation or abandonment trauma.[11] Here, death is not feared as a fact, but as a symbol of lived experience.

Less is known of the instance where death is welcomed, certainly by fewer psychologists than writers and poets. As Odier has demonstrated, analytic interpretations of the desire for death, either of the self or the loved one, have most often been distorted, due largely to theories of masochism determined *a priori*. For many abandonics, death is something other than destruction. It represents accomplishment: not a separation, but a union, tranquillity rather than torment. It is hard to imagine that religious belief does not play a prominent role here. It may seem natural enough that those who have been denied a life would seek one after death, but we note that the sense of a welcomed death is felt as keenly among those who have no religious convictions or philosophical assurances beyond this life. These feelings occupy a primitive domain, one closely linked to the magical belief that death is *the one* who creates all appeasement and reparation.

"Life would be unbearable", one analysand told me, "if it were not for the certainty that it will end."

Example 12: Extract from the journal of an abandonic in crisis:

> "All is worthless; inertia, whole hours pass to nothing. The conviction of a life irredeemably lacking, born from a jealousy of others: jaundiced. The immense consolation: death. Suicide is my lone sentiment of responsibility. A call to death, the ordeal of life is not eternal. The need to order my affairs: will, investments, household goods, books . . ., etc. I constantly say that I cannot support life if I cannot, at any moment, think of death. My hope is that this life be bankrupted."

For some of my analysands, Bach's the *Komme Süsser Tod* is of comfort during these bleak episodes. One told me she hums it every morning to find courage enough to face the day.

Many abandonics, who are not suicidal, become so with the onset of each abandonment anxiety crisis. They connect the bliss that the prospect of death brings to the bliss of an infancy where all of life's misfortunes, disappointments, and failures are wiped clean.

Example 13: During a severe abandonment crisis, a young woman who could not sleep visualised herself lying in a coffin. Each night, the fantasy was re-enacted. A significant detail: beneath her head was the little pink pillow from her baby carriage.

In analysing the dreams and fantasies associated with double death as compensation for the impossibility of life for either person, Odier has shown that the death wish for the object has the same beneficial element as the death wish for the self, especially if both wishes are joined, in reuniting forever those beings that life has separated and terrorised.

I will conclude here by mentioning certain abandonics whose security depends on possession of the loved being, but is not complete in death alone.

"To lose, is to possess forever in spirit" (Valéry, 1924, p. 76).

Certain of our patients subscribe fully to this affirmation. These are subjects for whom precious emotional relationships failed in reality, but they then go on to flourish in its absence, away from contingency and rivalry.

Example 14: This is the striking example of a special little girl loved by a tender and sensitive father, with a mother who was often and openly critical of her children, creating conflicts for the little girl. When she was eight, her father died; from then on she felt herself to be in close contact with him, so, when looking to the sky, it was with an intense feeling of communion, comprehension, and comfort. This feeling of possessing the absent father was total, without limit, sanction, or separation. The feeling was so profound that many years later it led to some dramatic developments in her life. Confident of a young man's affection whom she liked more than was realised, she risked letting him suicide, without lifting a finger or uttering a word to prevent it. This was the unconscious renewal of an old experience, the young's man death was to result in her total possession of him, as it had with her father's death, which she had never dared share with anyone.

CHAPTER TWO

Structures

Part I: Abandonic structure

Currently, in psychology, there is no problem more obscure and more discussed than *structure of the mind*. There have been theoretical attempts to create systematic models of the mind, but they are very different from each other and constituted of data that are difficult to grasp and even more so to organise. Within the study of psychology, the term "structure" itself contributes to diverse elements of the problem. In general psychology, essentially, psychic structure refers to the constitutional organisation of the ego, whereas in psychoanalysis the word "structure" has a much broader meaning because it encompasses unconscious psychic life as well, which is where we can explore and at least partially understand, particularly in terms of repression, how these are actively involved in the organisation of each individual's psyche. It is in this latter sense that the term "structure" will be used here.

Complexity of the data, and the overwhelming difficulty of establishing connections within that convolution, determines that the outlining of any psychic structure is a singularly delicate job. I do not shirk from such an undertaking but would like to minimise the difficulties, so this chapter has just one objective which, comparatively speaking, will make the task much easier: to provide an accurate description of the various psychological components that combine to generate abandonment neurosis. However, given the therapeutic concerns that have inspired this work, as well as the fact that, in terms of treating abandonment neurosis, detached observation and the recording of data is not enough, it becomes necessary, therefore, to connect the facts and construct hypotheses which, whether I like it or not, will inevitably lead to a degree of systematic modelling. In doing so, I will try to minimise the arbitrary by accurately defining each group of psychic forces outlined before then relating them to abandonic symptomatology.

We can, it seems to me, identify three distinct types of abandonic psychic structure. First is what I call the *simple* or *elementary abandonic*, in whom analysis does not detect an oedipal fixation, or a stable superego in the Freudian sense. This abandonic is governed by what I call the *bio-affective system of regulation*, designed solely to acquire and retain the emotional bonds indispensable to the abandonic, which are established in accordance with the loved object's personality and attitude, on the one hand, and the subject's primary need for security on the other.

Next is the *complex abandonic*, who has a psychic structure partially designed to meet the primary need for security, so the bio-affective regulation in this instance is only partly dominant. It has been inhibited by an entire system of prohibitions we also find in this abandonic, which varies in severity from one individual to another but generally has no sexual characteristics. So, the complex abandonic does have a type of superego whose origins will be discussed and about which we will formulate certain hypotheses.

Third is the *mixed abandonic*, who will, at times, present abandonic characteristics subject to the system of bio-affective regulation and prohibition, then alternately those of a superego formed by an Oedipus complex. For these patients, the abandonment occurred, or at any rate was constituted, as a neurosis on a date sufficiently advanced to allow an oedipal fixation that is not just recognisable but, because it is so infantile, needs to be clearly identified. It can be confusing for the analyst when the mixed abandonic first comes to treatment demonstrating these two causal strains of behaviour, one following primary bio-affective regulation together with the system of prohibitions which oppose it, and the other obeying an oedipal fixation—that we can call a secondary form of bio-affective regulation—which is being constrained by the intervention of a superego. The patient passes from one regime to the other, matching these interior phases to exterior circumstance. The cause of this change seems to depend on whether the abandonic is being rationed a dose of emotional security that is either more or less insufficient.

The elementary abandonic and the bio-affective system of regulation

This abandonic has the most primitive psychic structure of all and, as a consequence, exhibits behaviour that is the least socialised. Although there is aspiration and ambition towards adulthood, these patients remain, both emotionally and instinctually, in a state of infancy, totally incapable of meeting the demands of social adaptation. What immediately strikes us is the primacy of their affectivity over sexuality. However, this is an expression of affectivity very near to instinct, so very physically concentrated and linked closely to the need for security on every level of desire, making it inconceivable for this type of patient to create, or participate in, a loving adult relationship.

This biologically driven component, designed to sustain existence and life while simultaneously providing a diverse range of sensual pleasures, is closely connected to the affective needs of such a primitive developmental stage. One cannot exist without the other, which is why I have called these collective measures, which guarantee abandonic satisfaction of the fundamental need for security, the *bio-affective* system of regulation. By regulation, I mean the group of mechanisms always at the ready to defend and maintain the minimum level of necessary security. These compensatory mechanisms play a vital role in the fundamental equilibrium of the elementary abandonic.

Example 15: Mrs F is typical of the essential emotional state subject to bio-affective regulation. The analysis was limited in terms of sessions, so I could not tell if, eventually, it would reveal an oedipal fixation, but her history did provide a very powerful recollection, which left me in little doubt that the father, of diminished personality and often absent, had little impact on the patient's affective development, whereas the mother, by contrast, was a strong, albeit neurotic, character, unstable and unpredictable, inflicting upon the girl levels of expectation that could never be satisfied. Characteristically positive-attractive, her childhood and adolescence were spent exercising considerable ingenuity in trying to second-guess her mother in order to maintain the bond. Of very solid intelligence and endowed with good psychic intuition and suppleness, this patient has spent her life "catching the wind" in adapting to those she loves. Her bio-affective regulatory system is always alert, ready to intervene, make reparation, and, ultimately, prevent, or often save, desperate emotional struggles. The effort takes an enormous toll in terms of personal renunciation, required essentially to satisfy the need for security by constant adaptation to the object, done with a smile as if the demands of this internal quest caused her no pain and where, in fact, the patient considers the exactitude of little consequence, a small cost for a prize that is priceless: retention of the bond and of security. Her history also revealed that she never properly reached the genital stage, and, in contrast, was deeply susceptible to expressions of tender and sensual exchange. Men never existed for her, to the extent that only forthright, but tender, women could become erotic objects (see Chapter One, p. 14).

In the case of Mrs F, as with all elementary abandonic patients, another feature is the absence of an internal "legislature", or "critical agency". In other words, these subjects lack the defined hierarchy of values, even pre-morality values, which distinguish right from wrong and good from bad, that permit and defend, to various extremes, judgements that today encompass this and tomorrow that, depending on the episode and situation, but which are especially driven by the psychological need of maintaining a secure bond with the object. By contrast, the bio-affective system of regulation obeys no principles *a priori*, which is what leads us to conclude that there is an absence of a superego in the elementary abandonic, and not only in the Freudian sense, that is to say, derived from an Oedipus complex, but again also with the broader meaning we give that term as used in relation to the *complex abandonic* when we speak of a superego constituted according to a system of precise and rigid prohibitions.

These considerations are evidence of another structural component that characterises the elementary abandonic, which is an acutely enfeebled or quasi non-existent ego where psychic life has no elaboration and is confined entirely to sensibility. The normative sense of astonishment experienced by the individual, when a step is first taken towards constructive reflection in the face of interior contradictions or an absence of life direction, is foreign to the elementary abandonic. Such problems do not exist for them. They often claim to be intellectually lazy, but it would be more accurate to say that they only acknowledge "feeling". Thought, as such, is of no value because it is never apparent. Imposition of the impulsive sentiment deflects any motivation towards reflection. For the most part, it is not that these subjects are unintelligent, thus incapable of psychically constructing their lives, they simply have not reached, regardless of actual age and despite the frequency of broad or limited professional success, the developmental stage Piaget highlighted where the abstract concept of objective reasoning is acquired. This abandonic is only concerned with living the *affect*.

Being entirely preoccupied with material and affective security, this type of patient can ordinarily be appropriately compared to the infant. The difference between this subject and what we call normal individuals is immediately apparent and can often be the cause of great consternation to the latter, who are inevitably challenged when confronted by the former, especially if they become the object of abandonic affection with its vacuous solitude and lack of reciprocity.

If we consider the instinctual life of both elementary and complex abandonics, what strikes us is the primordial place their protective and defensive measures occupy, while sexual instinct remains of secondary importance.

By protective measures, I mean all behaviour that is also identifiable in a young animal attempting to maintain a sense of security when it searches for a presence or seeks proximity and contact through the need to nuzzle, nest, shelter, feed, guard against the elements, etc. Likewise, the abandonic invests enormous psychic energy into these types of behaviour to satisfy tactile and emotional needs that are of such primordial importance. If, on the other hand, reality looms and failure threatens this process, the abandonic will adopt a defensive position, the principal modes of which have been outlined in the previous chapter and can be expounded further by way of comparison with defence mechanisms of the other neuroses. So, we note that the more elementary the ego, the more primitive the mode of defence, whereas in the subject whose ego is more developed, we observe very subtle and elaborate defensive behaviours. Also, we find that the elementary abandonic's security measures, constructive or defensive, engage maximum instinctual energy.

The elementary abandonic will also resort to erotic pleasure as an additional defensive measure. However, if the subject must choose, these desires will be pushed aside in favour of the more primitive forms of satisfying the need for security. It is important here to distinguish between heteroeroticism and autoeroticism, because, for the majority of elementary abandonics, masturbation either has never existed or has been abandoned as unsatisfactory. Which is to say that in most subjects sexual eroticism is little prized. Often in its place is an oral sexuality, which manifests in the form of gluttony, the need to suck, chain-smoke, etc., corresponding to the infantile stage at which the subject remains fixed. Heteroeroticism, by contrast (tenderness, love, and sexual caress to a greater or lesser extent), is generally desired by this abandonic as proof of a love bond, but satisfaction is at least as affective as it is physical, and partners will often reproach the abandonic for being too emotionally focused.

Genital function in these subjects is problematic, so generally sexual life seems to have little or no value and sometimes serves only as a means of acquiring security. Although there are instances where sexual activity is overvalued and sought out, most often, to the contrary, it is felt as a threat, so abhorred. This is particularly true among females, for whom sexual relations are felt at best to be drudgery or at worst offensive and injurious because the male, in taking his pleasure, fails to consider her displeasure, thereby creating deep resentment through making evident the "lack of love" which augments anxiety and feelings of abandonment.

As I have said, we do not detect in these subjects anything characteristic of a superego. Effectively, this absence is not in the name of taboo or any kind of prohibition. Sexual relations are felt as abominable because the individual is still fixed in infancy, so has not evolved to the stage of erotic differentiation. The vehemence with which they will reproach a spouse's sexual desire is, most often, an emotional rather than a moral objection. This type of analysand will often insist: "If he loves me he would understand and be tender, give the kisses I love, and not demand those things that mean nothing to me."

Although reactions such as these are common in females, we also encounter them in the male of this type, particularly when partnered by a woman with normative levels of sexual desire.

There is much to be said regarding abandonic sexual behaviour. The topic merits specific study, as long as it remains the cause of suffering and failure within human relationships. Both men and women feel the negative effects of how emotional disquiet prevents relaxation: "He [or she] watches me all the time!" patients tell us.

They make this observation, of course, in the search for reassurance that their partner is "emotionally present". It then becomes a horrendous moment for the abandonic when the physical pleasure takes over and the spouse becomes "emotionally absent". I have found a number of women who have an irrepressible urge to speak when this happens, nothing of particular importance, but something that will cause distraction, thus interrupting the man's pleasure. Here again, this is not, it seems, an act of symbolic castration prompted by envy, but, rather, it is generated by anxiety in response to the prospect of abandonment by the object in favour of physical pleasure. For many abandonics, of whatever type and developmental stage, this pleasure in isolation represents a rupturing of the bond. This is because the question of sexual synchronicity and simultaneous orgasm is, for them, of central importance.

These matters go beyond the point, however, because they do not address the immediate issues, which are that elementary abandonic women are generally frigid and the men impotent, or, at least in the vast majority of cases, there is very little inclination towards genital orientated sexuality. However, for reasons already outlined, this absence is not experienced as personal deprivation. The subject usually only suffers indirectly, through having a partner at a more developed stage with the corresponding advanced level of sexual desire. Here, abandonics are often reproached and made at least partially aware of their deficiency; in addition, more importantly— and this is the cause of their greatest pain—it becomes a barrier to understanding and love.

Because this abandonic has not reached the stage of erotic differentiation and his or her need for tender devotion remains primal, the female, in particular, greatly values both pre- and post-coital expressions of tenderness. Many never feel quite ready for sex and much prefer the shared affection of foreplay or, in the case of those least developed, simple caresses passively received, which thereby become possession itself. They also feel it very important to know that the man has rejoined them after intercourse. For the elementary abandonic, this is the sole consolation taken from what is otherwise utter degradation.

Overall, abandonics fixed at the more primitive stages of development tend not to become spontaneously involved in heterosexual relationships, but if they do follow this path, usually it is to satisfy the desires of an object more closely aligned to a normative state than themselves. However, because they are neither attracted to nor interested in the sexual act, they are inept in the role, eventually finding in this environment more pleasure in those activities that lie alongside. Ill will usually results, and the sex life of such couples becomes the source of ongoing conflict.

In fact, it is rare that an abandonic patient, of whatever stage or type, does not recount, if not a life of exclusive homosexuality, then one where it has been at least episodic. In the female, the search for the mother, as analysts well know, frequently involves fixation on a same gender object for the satisfaction of erotic desire and the need for love. In the male, there is also need of a mother's love rather than a man's, but where the subject is a "newborn" who, through identification, becomes characteristically passive and feminine. In either case, the oedipal function involving primary object choice, as first illuminated by Freud, is reinforced here through the observation of abandonics. Not as oedipal in terms of choosing a sexual object, but, rather, pre-oedipal, evidenced in the more primal kind of love that is craved by both the elementary and the complex abandonic.

To summarise, the elementary abandonic presents three structural characteristics.

1. Bio-affective equilibrium is maintained by an unelaborate, but very sensitive and supple, system of regulation, which is directly dependent on the primary needs of security and love.
2. The ego, by virtue of being practically non-existent, is incapable of abstract reasoning, intellectually unmotivated, and, as a consequence, lacks order and cohesion.
3. Instinctual life is governed, along with all behaviour, through the bio-affective regulatory system of instinctual conduits, which provides security, defence, and an eroticism that can be more or

less sexual, but without ever having properly reached the genital stage.

The complex abandonic

These patients are frequently encountered in treatment and probably comprise the largest abandonic contingent. The complex type is also subject to the bio-affective system of regulation as outlined above, but the difference is that those characteristics do not exist in their pure state, so to speak, because the bio-affective regulatory system in this instance faces an important obstacle: a system of prohibitions.

I shall attempt to describe what this means, and then outline some hypotheses regarding the formation of these prohibitions.

First, as we have noted, there is a failure to detect in these subjects, even when analysed at length, any hint of attachments that are characteristically oedipal. In other words, at no time in their lives has a normative sexual object choice been made, and their psychology remains entirely dominated by a quest to find love embodied in the maternal image. Initially, this subject may seem to be a replica of the elementary abandonic already described. In fact, the two are extremely close in terms of biopsychic tendency and fundamental need, because the acquisition of security and love are pivotal to the psychological disposition of each. However, the complex abandonic, although also preoccupied with the pursuit of these same ends, escapes absolutely the totally instinctual, so non-elaborated, mentality of the elementary type. Is this difference due to some other psychosomatically constituted cause: an act of nature? Or is it the result of exogenous variables: environment, parental personalities, education systems, etc? I pose these questions as yet without answers because, at this point, my analytic data does not allow me to prefer one hypothesis over the other.

Whatever causes the necessary conditions for creation of these differences in the complex abandonic, observation confronts us with many cases where, despite oedipal derived superegos having failed to form, these patients are, none the less, tyrannised by mechanisms of prohibition no less severe that, at every turn, profoundly frustrate the subject's search to find love. What we do know is that in childhood both abandonic types observed and absorbed experiential facts from the immediate environment: parental and family attitudes, signs of approval and disapproval, means of seduction and offence, of pleasing and displeasing, etc. All this data allowed the child, desperate for love, to adapt behaviour at least to a certain degree, so averting, where possible, misunderstandings, blame, and exclusions while going in search of anything that favours contact and tenderness. However, it seems that the elementary abandonic cannot integrate this experiential data. The ego is only able to internalise the information very briefly, so that when there is a modification to the capricious environment, the subject will immediately adapt, changing security-seeking behaviour in accordance with the object deemed most likely to provide that security.

Complex abandonics, by contrast, fervently integrate experiential data and will bond with the adult from whom it emanates. Little by little, they elaborate and create, through successive identifications, what Freud called the ego ideal. We know how all-important this process is in the child, in terms of being the primary milestones that, in health, then evolve towards socialisation and formation of a morality base, a superego, in other words, whose subsistent elements remain evocable and conscious in the ultimate development of an ethical conscience and personal ideal: the ego ideal.

In the complex abandonic, it seems that this evolution has been arrested and, regardless of actual age, the subject remains, for reasons we will seek to clarify, at the point where the ego ideal has formed, which becomes an extremely rigorous moral and security code. This is, it seems to me, what gives rise to the system of prohibitions about which we have spoken. The complex abandonic can always be linked to particular beings—influential family members—who have played a pivotal role during the subject's infancy, and analysis generally has no difficulty identifying the person being emulated. Conversely, it is often a lot more difficult to liberate patients from their more conventional oedipal driven superego. We can ask if the reasons for this are due to the fact that abandonic prohibitions are conscious, whereas those of the superego are not. In the latter, we know the paradox remains unconscious because the ego constantly works and reworks that which depends on its jurisdiction and control, so here we see how the building of successive rationalisations has occurred over the years, founded on unpalatable parts of the ego ideal, which is able to exert the authority needed to prevent their otherwise normal integration into consciousness where they can be rejected. In treatment, we find that this is a place we run hard up against because it is strongly defended. By contrast, all the oedipal processes that cross the threshold into consciousness, thereby allowing analytic interpretation, despite being strongly resistant, at least offer the ego the privilege and novelty of analytic revelation. This is because these processes have not been the object of rationalisation, so sometimes can provide true catharsis for the subject. Many adults acquire a more critically objective view of their oedipal behaviour and enslavement to an ego ideal, which they have come to view wrongly as integral to themselves. It is from here, in part at least, it seems to me, that flows the force and resistance of the complex abandonic prohibitive systems which concern us. We shall see directly that there are also other causes of this resistance.

The complex abandonic poses a vexing problem for us: why and under what conditions do the pre-oedipal identifications assume the binding and disturbed characteristics that we observe in patients fixed to this kind of ego ideal? Here, we can examine various hypotheses,[12] and it is instructive to consult Odier at this point, who illuminates the meaning of more general observations that I have witnessed specifically in my own patients of this type.

These observations identify an established primary code that becomes rigid and restrictive under the following conditions:

1.   When it involves feelings of distress and suffering.
2.   When there has developed in the child a profound sense of enfeeblement, inferiority and failure to meet expectation, which is linked to feelings of danger, and when, for various reasons, there is a non-identification with the equivalent loss of love but where, on the other hand, such identification is impossible.
3.   When it is accompanied by anxiety.

Echoing Odier's views, we find that the infant's relationship with the frustrating object, whether it be the mother, father, or substitutes who have not met the basic needs for security and love, features precisely the three necessary conditions I have just specified: suffering, powerlessness (accompanied by an inner obligation to identify), and anxiety.

Example 16: Mr T is an intellectual of subtle and nuanced thought. Even as a child, the intelligence and subtlety of his comments were noted. His father, a man of equally strong intelligence, died, leaving his young son in the care of a mother who, although full of good intentions, was timorous, shallow, and had no real understanding of her son; in desperate need of care and attention, the boy clung to his mother, totally identifying with her in an attempt to please in return for love, all the more inexorably as his own intelligence and critical judgement came to contradict the way he wanted to see this maladjusted woman, to the point where the truth could no longer be ignored. Yet, the fear of losing love prevailed and made the adolescent, then the man, a non-existent being, a complete captive of the fears, defences, and interdictions resulting from this desperate maternal identification. Impotence and masochistic homosexual perversion crowned the work of this destructive identification.

Example 17: Miss S, aged twenty-five, raised by her parents to be "principled", aloof, conventional, and unemotional, suffered a total lack of solicitude and kindness. In open revolt against her parents, she finally left the family home, but carrying profoundly introjected commands, defences, and terrors that scarred her during childhood, leaving her incapable of constructing a life because she remains obsessed, preoccupied by "what was done and what was not done!" Despite having behaved so appallingly, the parents remain for this young woman, through their social function and moral standards, an ideal from which she cannot escape. The contrast is striking between her scathing, rebellious judgements on the one hand, as she recounts the facts of the parents' behaviour towards her, and, on the other, a sense of admiration for her incapacity, which she speaks about in a general, theoretical way, to live up to their lofty life principles.

It seems good identifications from emotionally generous parents actually have as their object the parents' ego. However, as Freud observed, an infant will often look beyond the parental image to another, which becomes idealised, and is, in fact, the parental superego. It is here, I believe, that the mechanisms of identification are painful and create the imprint that has such disastrous repercussions. These events occur on the basis of a parental belief that the infant is at fault, a disappointment, but the child will not be party to the belief because, for the child, it represents parental failure, which is synonymous with the loss of security, so the parents become what the child wants them to be rather than what they actually are. We note here that parents of this type often have very active superegos. These negative identifications are tenacious, and to combat them an enormous unconscious defence is required from the infant against himself or herself: one part aimed against reasoned critical judgement,[13] the other against an insatiable desire for retaliatory aggression and revolt. However, these emancipatory elements are elsewhere held in check by the guilt they generate and anxiety born of fear that the bond could eventually rupture.

The abandonic's familial environment, by definition, is dominated by a, or the, frustrating object, about whom the subject has retained extreme ambivalence and whose image, we note in the analysis, the patient continues to obsess over through the expression of profound thoughts and actions. Residing in this fixation is the essential cause of the prohibitive systems we have observed in the complex abandonic.

Note, however, that the subject's depression, accompanied by feelings of inadequacy and anxiety, is not produced uniquely through the primary object of frustration, but also often by the secondary rival object. The oedipal example is classic. We now need to consider this with regard to the *mixed* type, and, in particular, highly problematic cases involving females where there exists a doubling of prohibitions which censor rival object incest through a privation of love from that self-same object. Here we see that two mutually exclusive stages and mentalities can sometimes be confused, giving rise to fantasies, dreams, and behaviours that are, on occasions, abandonic and at other times oedipal. So here, success of treatment depends on the analyst clearly distinguishing these two causal elements as each comes into play.

The mixed abandonic

The mixed abandonic is the most difficult to identify. He or she is also the one for whom traditional methods of neurosis classification are shown to be the least adequate. For this reason, the therapist needs to closely scrutinise the precise psychic structure of any patient who presents with possible mixed abandonic type symptoms before embarking on an appropriate course of treatment.

Whether there is an abundance of evidence that an emotional disorder is oedipal in origin, or linked with an earlier infantile conflict connected to the need for love and security, is an issue which has attracted more and more attention in recent years from psychologists and psychotherapists. To my knowledge, however, there has been no previous study on the coexistence of both factors in a single subject. Research has revealed that this coexistence frequently occurs in cases where traumas of frustration are produced after the psychological transformation has been initiated by an oedipal phase. Here, the precise moment of abandonment, or, at least, the occasion when this trauma was first felt and neurotically elaborated, is vital to identify. However, it would be wrong to assume *a priori* that abandonment occurred after the age of four to five, thereby implying the child had passed through the oedipal transformation. In recent years, studies have demonstrated that there is an incidence, far more common than Freud first supposed, of oedipal lack in children due to a range of factors. Among these factors, the abandonic constitution, about which we shall speak in the following chapter, certainly, according to my observations, plays a primary role. So, if an abandonment neurosis seems to have appeared after the normal age of oedipal onset, it by no means follows that an Oedipus complex has been negotiated. By the same token, if a subject demonstrates predominantly abandonic symptoms, we should also be sceptical and cautious, and not settle on this diagnosis prematurely.

This reservation made, we must, none the less, be mindful of cases where both an oedipal and abandonment presence play simultaneous roles in the structure of a neurosis which, to the surprise of an unsuspecting analyst, unfolds and manifests following these two causal strains, switching from one to the other depending on internal phases. During periods where the subject is totally lacking in security, the abandonic element dominates. If the ego then stabilises and self-affirms, the oedipal material reappears. Often, the two interweave, producing radical behaviours, dreams, fantasies, and complexes that defy definition without a thorough knowledge of the subject's present life.

Here again, a patient presenting an abandonment neurosis can equally lead us to cast doubt over the existence of an oedipal component. Indeed, the entire abandonic mentality opposes an oedipal presence, but, of course, this mentality does not date back to the original abandonment trauma. Abandonment becomes traumatic if it encounters a particular terrain acutely intolerant of emotional frustration. That is to say, a child who makes an oedipal thrust is prone to falling into abandonment neurosis if circumstances of familial life are frustrated by an absence of love and security. As a result, the oedipal thrust will lack the normal clarity and breadth it assumes in the evolution of an emotionally healthy individual.[14] In this sense, affective love always dominates over sexual love, often with the latter never even becoming manifest. It seems that a consequence of the oedipal advance is the child attempting to differentiate from the parent of opposite gender, thereby beginning to make proper affirmation of masculine or feminine characteristics, but under the constant threat that such differentiation could result in loss of the object and isolation.

Child analysts, at times, observe this powerful conflict. It oscillates between, on the one hand, the rush of amorous love from a daughter to her father or little boy to his mother, initiating the development of a new affective attitude and behaviour as evidence the differentiation is operative, and, on the other, the alternative need for primal security which marks a return to the former identification. These two positions draft the emotional template to be lived later in adulthood, which are the primary and instinctual attitudes of fusion with the loved object. It is instructive to take note of these vacillations and the anxiety that precedes their regression.

Example 18: A female analysand of mine, who, as a child was subjected to the privation of security caused by parental neurosis, as a five-year-old made an oedipal advance, and recounted the following: the father, entering his study one day, was greeted by his adorned, well dressed little girl, who set about seducing him; he reciprocated the felicitous embraces and kisses, saying things to the effect of, "You're a lovely little lady who makes me truly cheerful." But the little girl's sweet diminutive face darkened with disquiet and, tearing off her clothes, she rushed into the arms of her father repeating, "I'm your little baby! I'm your little baby!"

Many memories recounted by adult abandonics of the mixed type are evidence of these shifts from one position to the other, often accompanied by anxiety. I do not think, for my part, given the context of these observations (regression to insecurity and desire, fear of autonomy because it is confused with solitude, affection dominated by the search for unity and fusion), the shifts represent unconscious guilt from a nascent Oedipus complex. Rather, everything leads me to conclude that it is a refusal by the ego to venture further down the path of differentiation, personal insight, and autonomy, because these are developmental processes that awaken in the subject the fear of isolation and loss of love.

This is why we can suppose, it seems to me, that, in such cases, what opposes the oedipal advance is the ego, and not the superego, which is rendered less necessary and so has barely formed because of the very low level sexual presence in this type of oedipal tendency. From here, hesitant oedipal attachments arise that are always ready for regression back to the primary need for love.

These general observations about the oedipal problem in the mixed abandonic are found regardless of gender. However, clinical work has allowed us to clarify particular points if we make certain distinctions between male and female subjects.

A girl abandonic, for example, will not form an oedipal attachment to a father who is himself fixed to the vacillating hesitancy of both positions just described. By contrast, the tender, sensitive father, possessing feminine characteristics, who likes to cuddle, pamper, and fulfil his child's need to be cared for, will alone foster an attachment to this small abandonic. From the very beginning, this type of "feminine" father simply plays the role of a substitute mother. Then, when the father becomes the object of oedipal love, these primary attributes, when retained, remain precious sources of security for his child. So, as the daughter moves into adolescence, she will continue the attachment with her father as this very young child. Later, as an adult, her relations will maintain these infantile characteristics and her preference will be for men who are emotionally sensitive, rather than those resembling the virile father figure who accentuates sexual difference, reviving in her the fear of isolation.

For the same reason, an abandonic girl will turn away from a distinctly masculine and strong father, who remains for her a stranger that she will always more or less fear. In this instance, an oedipal inversion will prevail, as she remains fixed solely to the mother figure, the father being regarded as an intruder and proximate rival. There is a strong prospect that an identical scenario will be reproduced later in life if, despite her resistances, she marries and her husband remains alienated as someone who cannot be integrated into her life. In contrast, the mother, or a female substitute, plays the primary role, and it is to her that all the profound abandonic affectivity is directed.

In certain cases, where the father's character has favoured an oedipal attachment in an abandonic daughter, we then see the mother embody two prohibited domains: first, the threat that security will be frustrated through loss of love, given that she is the child's primary object; second, because she is the father's wife, whose place it is forbidden to take. Here, the analyst is confronted by patient fears, inhibitions, and guilt from dual origins: one attached to a primitive identification with the frustrating object, the other, more recent, created by the prohibition of incest. Experience has shown that when these phenomena arise and there is failure to search for their actual causes, especially if the analytic material is assumed to be the exclusive domain of an Oedipus complex—the causal factor with the greatest bio-psychic charge seems to be the most primitive, which is to say, linked to the primary need for security rather than the Oedipus complex—then the analysis cannot liberate the patient from either of these prohibitions. In fact, on the contrary, they will be reinforced.

With regard to males, the conjunction of oedipal phenomena and abandonment anxiety creates in this version of the neurosis a structure that is much more complicated. If, as a child, the male directed love to the opposite sex, his mother, then, as an adult consistent with that choice to his wife, his emotional development faces less difficulty than that of the female mixed abandonic. This seems to hold true in some respects, at least, and has often been highlighted, which, in contrast to the female, makes understanding the psychology of masculine abandonment neurosis relatively difficult, particularly in regard to the mixed type. Essentially, this is because it is often very problematic identifying the precise factors that influence a boy's attachment to his mother and that distinguish the flow he directs to her as a secure protector from those aimed at her as the primary feminine image.

To establish with any certainty the various contingencies through the clinical course of such cases, because there does indeed seem to be several different types, very extensive analytical research material needs to be gathered, supplemented by direct observation from the age of oedipal onset until puberty, of demonstrably abandonic boys. In the current absence of such data, I shall confine myself here to some hypotheses that will need to be tested for verification. In addition, I am hopeful that these comments will arouse the interest of other analysts.

One observation that seems certain is that all masculine subjects who suffer abandonment neurosis present a passive masochistic fixation on the mother, which can vary to every degree of intensity. This seems to be the foundation stone upon which the rest of the neurosis is built and is the element that other factors come to combine with in various dosages, the Oedipus complex being one of them.

Of the complex abandonic type, those who feature the systems of prohibition and are lacking any oedipal presence (from where the bulk of my observations are drawn because most of my male patients fall into this group), the clinical picture is roughly summed up as a passive masochistic fixation to the mother. There is no detectable phallic phase and no masturbation. Homosexuality, either latent or realised in the passive role, is carried to adulthood. In either case, there is penile insensitivity, except in the case of masochistic homosexual fantasy, where erection is achieved but not ejaculation. Here, the mother is both the frustrating and castrating object, and she emanates all systems of prohibition.

So, in the mixed abandonic type, what becomes of the Oedipus complex on the basis of this passive, masochistic reaction to the frustrating mother? What might at first seem surprising is that an Oedipus phase could be produced at all under such conditions. But what should be noted here, on the one hand, is the great diversity of external circumstances that can trigger abandonment anxiety, including the very broad and varied types of frustrating mothers, and, on the other hand, the child's psychosomatic domain and the greater or lesser strength of ego it has to combat the neurosis. I believe the most unfortunate outcome is where emphatically traumatic circumstances have occurred which result in the absence of any oedipal presence in the child, so that the subject will present as a clear clinical picture of the complex abandonic type already described. Under slightly happier circumstances, where there is an unstable, sometimes angelic and other times demonising mother who is the emotional equivalent of a Scottish shower running hot then cold, a constitutionally less fragile boy will emerge, where oedipal phases will alternate with those of abandonment anxiety. Between these two extremes, every nuance is free more or less to apply processes of differentiation and affirmation of an oedipal derived self.

As I have said, an abandonic constitution will oppose oedipal admission, which seems to me indisputable, certainly in the case of female subjects. In the boy, however, such an assertion calls for some additional comment. We can observe that when the mother is not inherently frustrating—so where her son has not developed a disposition profoundly masochistic through fear of abandonment—that the boy is drawn to her, favouring a rapport which is more or less amorous, with erotic kisses and caresses that lean biologically towards the oedipal. In my opinion, however, this form of occasional eroticism is too superficial, so does not involve any great change in the boy's attitude, which remains essentially passive. His mother's quest, which is to conquer him, does not really alter either, or that of his father, who is demonstratively virile and a combative rival in the true oedipal sense.[15] It seems that in many cases the bio-affective problem of this developmental phase only serves to reinforce the desire for "anchoring" with the mother. Yet, simultaneously, it gives that dependence a slightly different appearance, which can be confusing when, in fact, the boy's affectivity continues to be regulated essentially by extreme passivity, the lack of security, and fear of losing his object. In my view, this frustrated oedipal push never crosses into the developmental stage that allows the boy a pathway to awareness of masculinity and strength, which is all work that remains to be done.

With regard to the development of individual psychic structure and the construction of neurosis, it seems to me that, by excessive extension of the term *Oedipus complex*, the expression of facts, feelings, and strongly differentiated impulses can become confused with each other.

Freud, who was obliged to modify his initial observations that the oedipal phenomenon was the crux of all neurosis, eventually attached great importance to the pre-oedipal stage, particularly in the female. He came to ask if, in women, there might be a phase of exclusive primary attachment to the mother that extended far beyond what was previously supposed, and could perhaps hamper transition to the masculine object, sometimes to the point of an impasse.

The question of distinguishing between oedipal and pre-oedipal material, it seems to me, invariably brings us to Freud's observation that oedipal onset essentially marks a change of instinctual direction in the child, as is seen in girls, and not simply a change of object.

In my view, this is why it is impossible to agree with assertions put forward in the conclusion of the paper, otherwise so lively and evocative, presented by Behn-Eschenburg at the psychoanalytic conference in Wiesbaden during 1932, where he said: "The fewer signs analysis gathers of an Oedipus complex, the earlier this complex played its role in the neurosis."[16]

Other analysts, Melanie Klein prominent among them, also subscribe to this view. For Behn-Eschenburg, the age of four or five years, being generally considered the oedipal age and in boys the phallic phase at its height, runs contrary to the facts. According to him, the oedipal onset often occurs much sooner, as much as two and three years earlier, at an age, he himself concedes, where it is impossible for the child to achieve the all-important genital stage and maintain it at that level, even momentarily.

To speak of this as an oedipal age, when children are still negotiating narcissistic, oral, and anal phases, would seem contradictory. Without doubt, the girl of this age can, for a variety of reasons, and not only for having an awareness of her absent penis, for which she has rendered the mother responsible, turn away from her mother and attach to the father. Many educational factors and familial events can contribute to such a shift. It does not follow, however, that here we can speak of an oedipal shift in the true sense, that is to say, with a change of object *and* instinctual purpose. I believe it is extremely rare that two- or three-year-old girls attempt to please and seduce their fathers, psychically at least, in order to fulfil the role of a small woman. More generally, the child of this age who fixes upon the father in search of support, consolation, and tenderness does so because these qualities, for one reason or another, are lacking in the mother. Bonding with the father under these circumstances does ultimately, of course, take on great importance in the girl's development, but I think in a manner more detrimental than favourable. This is because she has changed her object without changing her instinctual purpose. Consequently, there will be a high risk that this mechanism will continue to intervene later in life through preferences for masculine attachments that mirror her primary purpose in choosing the father, so will always remain, in effect, the relationship between a man and a little girl.

One striking fact that merits noting is that generally, after eight to ten months of treatment, fresh oedipal material appears in the analysis of both the male and female abandonic. After the problem of abandonment has been carefully analysed and the patient has been liberated from the infantile fixations and passivity which the abandonment created, the analyst then assists with a modification in the analytic material the subject brings concerning the parent of the opposite sex, regardless of that parent being dead or alive. Through dreams and fantasies, the analysis more or less abruptly now comes to express much more marked oedipal characteristics, accompanied by a developmental growth of femininity in the female and masculinity in the male.

Why was this oedipal push retarded? What was its origin? These questions need to be considered. Is it the resurgence of an oedipal fixation that was thwarted by the anxiety of abandonment and so remained latent? Or is the subject experiencing a first amorous attraction to the parent of opposite gender, having been liberated from that anxiety, making it possible and appropriate to pursue an emotional relationship within the sexual differentiation? What role in the manifestation of these new instinctual and affective manifestations, which attest to a developmental advance, did the relationship between analyst and analysand play? We know this relationship constitutes in itself, for most abandonics, an extraordinary experience: a stable, non-threatening relationship where the patient is accepted and understood, usually for the first time in his or her life.

In this area, there are many barriers to understanding which are compelling for a range of reasons, but which remain problematic. However, in my view, the powerful emotional experience that constitutes analytic treatment, counteracting distrust and the multitude of abandonic fears, is a vital factor in the subject's affective maturation. Analysis allows these steps to be taken, which previously the patient dare not attempt for lack of security.

Would not this first experience of a safe and secure environment, due both to the analytic work and the continued understanding of an uncritical analyst, prompt the subject to resume development from the point of its failure, and persevere step by step until maturity is won? This view accords with my own experience and has led to formulation of the following hypothesis: the appearance of an oedipal phase during treatment is a revival of what previously was a repressed trauma.

The subsequent interior evolution that marks and accompanies development of a stage never before reached seems to support this view. However, this raises a problem of ontogeny which is beyond both the scope of this work and the author's competence.[17]

Whatever interpretation we give to the oedipal phase of treatment, it marks a turning point in the patient's evolution. In elementary and complex abandonics, this represents a new acquisition. In the mixed type, it marks the transition from frustrated oedipal desire to a true oedipal phase where there exists a fusion between the idea of relationship and choice.

Part II: Other structural components of abandonment neurosis and structural comparisons

In the first part of this chapter, I have attempted to specify the particular psychic structure that typifies abandonment neurosis, and also to demonstrate that it is founded on an abandonic constitution which generates anxiety and insecurity sparked as a result of frustration.

The precise description of this structure would remain incomplete, however, if we did not now envision construction of the neurosis on the basis of abandonment. This is to say, those libidinal and psychological factors that we know intervene at the different stages of childhood and which combine with the abandonic component to create this specific syndrome.

Moreover, the need to identify and differentiate this syndrome naturally leads to comparisons with others that it might be mistaken for initially. So, in the second part of this chapter, I shall make this differentiation as well as completing the description of abandonic structure, the basic tenets of which have already been outlined.

Abandonment neurosis and other neuroses with diverse structural combinations

Anxiety, its nature and form

We have emphasised that anxiety is so prominent among the symptoms of abandonment neurosis as to constitute its starting point. However, the term is applied in so many diverse ways, it is necessary to clarify exactly the meaning it is being given here. It might, indeed, surprise some to know that the word "anxiety" is also used to describe guilt, fear of castration, phobias, and infantile terror.

In cases of castration anxiety and, especially, guilt anxiety, we see that total intellectual elaboration has intervened, which means these processes must involve reason and judgement, however summary or erroneous. Both presuppose the existence of a superego and a conflict within the newly developing ego, able to grasp the opposition that pits instinctual requirement against familial demand.

Abandonment anxiety, in contrast, has all the characteristics of the early developmental stage to which it belongs. This is anxiety at its most primitive, bound to the incapacity of an infant to meet its own needs and defend against the threats of an exterior world. The experience is immediate and extremely disorientating, a deluge of emotion against which the ego is rendered helpless. During the second year, the child moves to a pre-logical infantile stage where magic predominates, a characteristic subsequently retained by the subject regardless of age. The process by which the self is gradually able to distinguish from the non-self, introjection and projection, provides the anxiety with infinite possibilities to extend and later to rationalise.

Even among the most intelligent and rational of adult abandonment neurotics, anxiety cannot serve as a "danger signal" as it does in other less primitive forms of anxiety. Gripped by the imminent menace of frustration, the abandonic immediately regresses to the state of primary impotence and the ego, overcome with emotion and fear, feels the full brunt and inevitability of the dreaded consummation.

It takes many months of analysis to guide a patient towards a perception that his or her nascent anxiety can be used as a warning, a call to awareness, in situations that involve external or internal danger. But what the ego is then able to achieve when the anxiety next surges is, first, a marked reduction of its intensity resulting from the analysis and, second, a strengthening of the ego itself.

Neurosis of abandonment and libidinal stages

Within the structure of abandonment neurosis, it seems necessary to distinguish between the intervention of libidinal drives at their different stages and the characteristic maladjustments that fixation by an individual on one or other of the libidinal phases produces. If we consider that the passage from oral to anal to genital stages constitutes normative individual development, the question remains: what degree of fixation on one or other of these states is the result of infantile trauma or temperamental predisposition? In the second case, we can assume that either an oral or anal fixation and the affective reactions that manifest as a result—greed and possessiveness, etc.— will be due to the same group of causes already identified in the individual's very nature.

Oral and anal fixation

Patient observation has demonstrated that those we categorise as positive-attractive are characteristically oral, while the negative-repulsive generally seem to be anal. However, here we can evidence oral fixation as the dominant, more pronounced element to a greater or lesser degree. This is because oral characteristics are always present in the abandonic clinical picture, by virtue of the mother remaining the centrepiece representing both oral and affective satisfaction.

However, this premise made, we can easily distinguish two groups within it: those actively seeking, although inadequately, satisfaction of their fundamental rapacity through both emotional and "oral" means, who are always ready to accommodate all possible pleasures in any field, while the other group remains in a general state of passive and suspicious "retention".

Of those manifestly fixed at an oral or anal stage, where the analysis has probed deeply but could detect no evidence of infantile trauma, we need to ask if there has not been a general exaggeration in the establishment of these libidinal fixations. In such instances, we are reduced to hypotheses such as: things happened as if . . . But is it justifiable in these cases to place emphasis on a fixation on a given libidinal state? Often, would it not be more appropriate to approach affective and instinctual life as facets at work on the same level, which is to say, from the point of view of them both being *needs*? For example, there is the need for emotional proximity and care, both for the clinging, cuddly child and for the one who refuses to stay on the pot and relentlessly pursues the mother, demanding her attention. The need for security and presence is manifest in every aspect of a child's life. Intrinsic to both of these examples are strictly affective and instinctual behaviours, which are relatively easy to detect analytically when there is no evidence of trauma. These basic needs alone seem to explain those issues thought to be libidinal, in terms of both physical and emotional life.

For my part, I believe it is frustrated emotional need, more so than erotic fixations at early stages of development, that holds the abandonic back from the genital stage. Analysis of oral and anal fixations in these neurotics results in the therapist being confronted with their emotional state and mode of loving, where possessive and captive tendencies work in contrast and opposition to the sharing emphasis of a genuine sexual stage.

This is why analysis of the characteristic anal behaviour in the abandonic does not reveal the same climate, if I may use that term, as it does with that of an obsessional neurotic. In the latter, we know anal fixation covers a powerful aggressive dynamism which may extend to sadism, and it is this sadism that constitutes a fundamental principle of the neurosis. The opposite applies in an abandonic. If there is an anal component that demonstrates aggression, it is usually in milder forms: opposition, negativism, suspicion, the need for revenge, etc. It is not sadism in any real sense, the passive element being, by contrast, more important.

Phallic phase

In the light of the aforementioned, it is also worth noting the frequent incidence of abandonic men who seem never to have experienced a phallic phase, or, if it did make an appearance, they immediately repressed it as a bodily function which, highlighting differentiation from the mother, risked separation from her.

The problem of castration

The problem of abandonic castration is posed not in relation to feelings of guilt, as with oedipal desire, but, rather, in the compulsion to have affective need fulfilled and the fear of losing love. For the satisfaction of these needs, no sacrifice, however vital, is too great.

In cases where the mother, who is a victim of her own neurosis, unconsciously detests the gender of her child, there is no other way—because there can be no risk of the exposure of abandonment—but for the child to disown itself. So, for example, when there is discord between the boy's gender and the mother's secret desires, a case more common than might be realised, the child is faced with a cruel dilemma: renounce either rapport with his mother or his own sexuality. So, the castration that we observe here results directly from fear of losing love.

In the male abandonic, it is often apparent that the cause of the mother's disquiet, his penis, is literally hated by the subject himself, so its function is completely inhibited. In girls, dealt frustration because they are not boys, this equivalent castration, less obvious and rarely noted, makes the quest to fully achieve a physical and mental sense of femininity no less profound.

The girl raised by a sensitive mother amid a predominately masculine familial environment, despite having acquired a sense of self-value, can, none the less, camouflage her femininity and sexual desires for fear that, as occurred with the mother, it will not attract male attachment. In these circumstances, her feminine characteristics, rather than becoming an integral part of self-worth, constitute a threat to love.

When guilt is added to this emotional mix, we know—as the result of educational intervention and prohibition, albeit rudimentary, of oedipal desire—the abolition of sexuality is never more rigorous or more unconsciously motivated and complex. Superego censorship then lends powerful support to affective fear. However, to me, the point that seems to be most important here is that fears linked to the loss of love alone are sufficient to provoke the sense of physical and psychic castration, so if analysis of these fears is not managed with care, these elements of the superego will remain malformed, thereby subjecting the abandonic to do their bidding.

In summary, it appears that for a particular category of child, and, therefore, of neurotic adult also, instinctive life lacks the extreme requirements that fulfil the needs for affective security and love. The analyst might be a little surprised to observe the incredible investment poured into anything that helps secure the relationship with the object—the mother or her substitute—and, in contrast, the profound absence of investment into the first instinctually driven manifestations of individual life. It would seem that these patients mostly sacrifice the physical aspect of biological need in favour of the affective aspect of biological need, with regard to dependence on others.

Abandonment neurosis and psychotic states

Certain patients demonstrate particular manifestations of abandonment neurosis that can give rise to diagnostic confusion. In the realm of psychiatry, for example, because there is a predominance of habitual psychosis among some patients, we can tend to paint a clinical picture that suggests, in those we would certainly classify as abandonic, combined elements common to both abandonment neurosis and certain psychotic states, before concluding, perhaps prematurely, in favour of psychosis. So, it is important here to highlight three principal points which demonstrate that the question of diagnosis is particularly delicate.

1. *Interpretations of masochism within abandonment neurosis, and paranoia*: we have seen the form and particular role affective masochism plays in abandonment neurosis, with the emphasis on the prominence of fantasy production in both positive-attractive and negative-repulsive categories, where the subject assumes the role of victim.

Despite a generally constructive and amiable disposition, the positive-attractive ego, infested with anxiety, cannot resist this type of delirium, as it provokes ideas of abandonment. The entanglement of painful emotions, catastrophic ideas, formidable suppositions, and fearful images that transform initial doubt into "reality" all psychically overflow, with each element reinforcing the others as a means of grasping control until the certainty of misfortune sets in and despair is finally triumphant. During these crises, all interpretations are possible, as betrayal and grief come to constitute the order of things.

With even greater conviction, the negative-repulsive, already inclined to see himself or herself surrounded by darkness, duplicity, and choking resentment, succeeds in acquiring during these crises of anxiety perceptions of violence that are virtually limitless.

We are generally inclined to interpret such intense and absurd emotions as paranoid. Yet, in fact, there is much more opportunity here when, theoretically, in some cases of abandonment neurosis, we are confronted by patients in crisis. Because these crises are born, flourish, and terminate following the laws of cause and effect, which can be identified and understood as having a beginning and an end, generally the analyst can bring the crisis under control. If this does not happen at the outset, it is because the anxiety, which ultimately must be dissipated, has not begun to calm. How this crisis evolves and the effectiveness of analytic intervention towards its resolution are the first two key differences that indicate whether or not we are dealing with a case of abandonment neurosis or paranoia.

Another difference is constituted in the mobility of abandonic interpretation: the delirium's epicentre of betrayal, frustration, and abandonment certainly remains the same, but the facts from where these interpretations arise can have constant and infinite variation. It is as if—and this is what is observed—the reasons behind the fear are not important because the fear itself, the fear of self, provides every possible manifestation. Abandonic interpretation is never fixed; it does not have the two-dimensional appearance of paranoia.

There can be what looks like an exception to this rule in some cases of adolescent abandonment neurosis. The subjects are usually male, aged between twelve and twenty. At first, and often for some weeks, there seems to be, rather than an interpretative crisis, an impenetrable, chronic state of delirium that the analyst cannot control, where adolescent complaint and grievance can become violent and bear a closer resemblance to psychosis than neurosis. However, the adolescent abandonic is often, more so than the adult counterpart, in the grip of magical thought, to the point where interpretations relate more to primitive pre-causality than adult logic, so it is understandable that a therapist can often be disorientated by such a patient and feel powerless in the attempt to utilise a therapeutic method, such as analysis, which requires a minimum of collaboration. Above all, it is important to remember that, in the case of an abandonic, one characteristic will persist: the absence of fixed and rigid interpretations.

Experience has taught me not to rush, particularly when confronted by cases such as these, in formulating a diagnosis of paranoia. Bearing in mind the levels of mistrust and violence generated in this kind of adolescent resulting from frustration and other forceful mechanisms of defence, the analyst must take great care to find a chink in the subject's armour and establish initial contact. It is often useful to engage on the same level of magical thought where the patient will endlessly play out fantasy, and that way gently lead him or her gradually back to the reality that is so feared.

Cases where the above therapeutic efforts fail and we have no choice but to diagnose a state of constitutional paranoia beyond the means of this treatment are rare.

2. *Absence of real contact with others, isolation and the schizoid state*: this applies solely to the negative-repulsive. Positive-attractive affectivity immediately excludes any schizoid characteristics. Certain negative-repulsives demonstrate an indifference, or unemotionality, in

both speech and behaviour that might make us suspicious but the neutral tone is an attrition of the emotions evoked by their misfortune. The apathy with which they greet even positive analytic intervention is as if it concerns someone else. Every mode of colourless, amorphous reaction may be considered here the result of profound affective ravages. What is more, these patients generally live reclusively, isolated by their egocentricity and mistrust of others, so are incapable of participating in affective relations that are truly intimate because, above all, they fear any threat that might alienate their precious independence. Often negative-repulsives' anal characteristics will contribute to reinforcement and maintenance of their emotional defence mechanisms. These neurotic manifestations can appear with particular force at the outset of treatment, requiring the analyst to pose certain questions. Here again, what gradually allows establishment of diagnostic certainty are the non-permanent characteristics of these manifestations. They are not fixed. Often, over many months, the clinical picture of these patients, in terms of their relations with others, will remain dominated by the characteristics we have indicated, but the analyst will become able more frequently to unlock affectivity, allowing the appearance of emotional impulse through the expression of regrets and desires, etc., thus demonstrating the many obvious inhibitions hitherto preventing their employ in an otherwise normal affectivity.

3. *Structural flaws and constitutional debilitation in the elementary abandonic*: patients of this type pose a problem I can only outline here, because the data I possess are currently insufficient to provide a solution. The question posed is as follows: can the absence of order, cohesion, and elaboration in the elementary abandonic's psychic structure be due to the neurosis itself, through fixation at this primitive state of infancy, because the conflicts that took place were so intense? Or should we regard these subjects not as psychotic, strictly speaking, but as victims of a constitutional alteration in psychic function which has debilitated the mind and is characterised by the absence of instinctual, emotional, and moral organisation? Such are the questions that analyses of the elementary abandonic have raised, remain pending, and which, ultimately, I hope to resolve.

CHAPTER THREE

Aetiology

As we know, the formation of a neurosis involves the genesis and interaction of numerous causal factors, sometimes acting successively, sometimes simultaneously, gradually entrenching the subject's malady. In the previous chapter, I attempted to show how abandonic psychic structure evolves and is generated by abandonment anxiety on the one hand, to which is added, on the other hand, intervention of instinctual impulses and emotions that accompany the different stages of childhood development. This action is strongly modified, as we have seen, by the factors that initiated the neurosis, which are feelings of abandonment and the primary state of anxiety to which the subject is fixed.

In all neuroses, the effects of neurotic disturbance themselves become causal. Psychotherapy reveals this development where each element is born of its predecessor, and, in turn, transforms the individual's psychic terrain with its contribution to the vicious circle. Here, the aim of treatment is to break the circular process at its point of least resistance. This finding is particularly apparent in abandonment neurosis and, as is also the case with all physiological illness, this secondary aetiology in neurosis plays an important role that must not be neglected because it justifies, in part at least, neurotic complaint: feelings of inadequacy, inferiority, the incapacity to compete, etc., which is often objectively confirmed in the patient.

Leaving aside this second degree of causality, the importance of which has been highlighted, I propose in the remainder of this chapter to outline the primary causes of abandonment neurosis.

These, in my view, appear to be threefold:

1.   Infant constitution
2.   Emotional attitudes of the parents
3.   Abandonment trauma.[18]

In all abandonment neurosis, we can note that categories (1) and (2) alone are sufficient to rupture psychic equilibrium and produce the specific syndrome that is this neurosis. Category (3), in contrast, the trauma and anxiety generated by an abandonment, seems to hold a secondary position and its action, although not necessary in the formation of the neurosis, is generally reinforced by a defective family environment that agitates the particular characteristics of the individual who is unable to withstand such deprivations.

As we can observe, *infant constitution* plays an essential role in the aetiology of abandonment neurosis. This is the conclusion to which the therapist is drawn as more analytic experience is gained in the field. Whereas with other neuroses, the emphasis must be placed on trauma that triggered initial conflict within the individual who is otherwise regarded as having a more or less normative orientation, in abandonment neurosis, the problematic crux almost always resides in a constitutional predisposition which renders the individual incapable of adapting to the norm, condemning him or her to a state of chronic, morbid anxiety and feelings of worthlessness, without this particular life necessarily having been more difficult and dramatic than any other.

Precisely how is this constitutional state predisposed to abandonment neurosis? This is not an easy question to address and to keep within factual terrain I will limit my answer to a summary of observations that distinguish psychical from physical predisposition in the infant abandonic. Psychically, the infant contained within our adult patient and the infant directly observed experiencing abandonment anxiety present three characteristic traits:

1.   Strong affectivity, with a predominance of this need over other needs.
2.   An intensely possessive need of loved ones which, to a greater or lesser extent, is camouflaged; intolerance of privation; absence; and sharing.
3.   A definite tendency to anxiety.

Which came first, (1) or (3)? It is impossible to know precisely at this point if the emotional rapacity provoked the anxiety or *vice versa*. However, what we can say without doubt is that they co-exist, (1) being essentially psychical and (3) physical, and that each conditions the other as they drive together in tandem.

Both are observed in the newborn. The mothers recognise all of these *little difficulties* as they arise: hypersensitive reactions to the slightest change in vocal intonation or routine, every maternal absence either real or imagined, as with a simple distraction, for example. These reactions are felt with overwhelming acuity which provokes, apropos of nothing and everything, anxiety, if not fear. From the outset, these so called *difficulties* are recognisable as emotions capable of generating intense feelings where the satisfaction of love outweighs all other need, or, rather, where other pleasures primarily depend for their existence on the charge this emotional atmosphere creates. The parents know only too well that these children can never be appeased for paternal absence and affective deprivation by any gift offering or sweet treat. In contrast, gifts and bonbons are of enormous importance if they are given as a gesture of love, understanding, and tangible proof of an indestructible emotional bond.

This child abandonic embodies a type of emotional gluttony:[19] always demanding more, but never getting enough. To feel happy and at peace, there must be a surrounding entourage to love and cherish the subject, who will then return that love. Also, in general, nothing can be allowed to fracture familial equilibrium and, specifically, unity with the mother or her substitute, which provides the evidence for proof of her love.

Alternatively, all that would menace unity and undermine this exclusive bond triggers despair and revolt. Here, security unravels with the same ease that saw its foundation. Everything depends entirely on the atmosphere constructed around the subject. This climate is often created with great attention to detail and nuance, things another child, a brother or sister perhaps, would find trifling. It also risks going entirely unnoticed by an inattentive adult. Learning adaption to life's demands is relatively easy when it touches nothing emotional, but this is not the abandonic child's primary interest, which is an almost complete intolerance of anything that implies a renunciation of possessive love. This intolerance is a mentality that characterises the abandonic's entire life.[20]

It appears to me that the manifest anxiety we are identifying in these infants sits on the border separating the psychical from the physical. This always testifies, it seems, to a functional disturbance triggered in the abandonic by a threat to security and the need for love, which must be the gravest form of this disturbance, whereas its least severe manifestation can be seen as a necessary condition, a latent state of anxiety to which we are all psychically predisposed.

According to my observations, the abandonic is also usually physically compromised. Without encroaching too far on a medical field not well known to me, I can attest to the broad number of abandonic patients who suffer from autonomic disorders. In fact, its action appears to be the consequence of a general law so apparent that it cannot be ignored. Anxiety generates autonomic imbalance that produces very acute secondary symptoms of physical instability and insecurity. So, it follows that physical insecurity becomes a symbolic reality of affective insecurity, and between the two domains alternate escalating themes are applied and played out. With all the trouble and pain that is the neurological lot of autonomic imbalance, which generally medicine is unable to relieve, abandonment neurosis does have a beneficial side, due largely to its masochism. This is where the patient, unaware that physical constitution plays such an important role in the genesis of this neurosis and its subsequent misfortunes, sees the physiological ailments that he or she is beset with as resulting entirely from the psychological frustrations and sorrows that have been suffered.[21]

Among the manifestations of autonomic disorder frequently observed in the abandonic are all gastrointestinal strains, including enteritis. Here again, the child is often subjected to interactions between the physical sensation of emptiness and the sense of enfeeblement that follows bouts of diarrhoea, which is symptomatic of dependence, the need for care and love. Sometimes, strong diarrhoeic episodes are experienced by the infant in panicked terror, for fear of death, as if the body is disintegrating, rapidly being reduced to nothing. Deeply affected by such physical trauma, these children cling to their familial surround claiming an emotional compensation overwhelmingly believed to be their right.

Briefly described, these are the principal psychical and physical constitutional factors that take precedence in the aetiology of abandonment neurosis. On to this psychosomatic foundation, the educational components are next considered, in particular *the emotional attitudes of parents to their children*. What I have said regarding infant predisposition is sufficient to demonstrate adroit and intuitive intellect in cases where development looks normative. So, it is also completely legitimate to ask, in the event where this has failed to occur, if such infantile emotional gluttony, incapable of self-sacrifice and wracked by anxiety, does not, by necessity, evolve into this neurosis.

It would be tedious and unnecessary to review the various psychological contingencies that create a familial life where psychic security has no privilege of place, and which, on the contrary, creates a troubled, disturbed environment where the infant searches in vain to have primordial need satisfied. Such a study would require examination of all the parents' problems, both as individuals and as a mother and father. All psychotherapists and analysts, of children in particular, are familiar with the diverse causes and heavy consequences that hinder or render ineffective and clumsy the love of parents for their children.

There are, however, two connected points of evidence that must be presented here. The first concerns the distinction between different kinds of abandonics, some being much more susceptible in terms of ulterior childhood development than others. The second raises a problem of the individual's primary feelings of value, and his or her relationship with being an object worthy of love and solicitude.

Analytic experience shows, in effect, that the infant, in spite of being confronted with stark reality, demonstrates an extraordinary sensibility to intention and is particularly attuned to registering every nuance of feeling to which it is subjected. When we reflect on such striking observations, clearly they merit a more controlled and systematic study. The greater a child's affective endowment, the more acute the sensibility to profound and erratic parental attitudes, conscious or unconscious, which is to say, this infant type is more predisposed to abandonment neurosis, the potential affective intensity of which we have already stressed.

It is from this point that children react in very different and subtle ways to their relative solitude and deprivations of solicitude and care. These are measured according to levels of frustration generated, and whether or not they are objectively justified. For the child, the whole question hinges on knowing if the privation has an external cause totally unconnected to the parents or the self, but to which the former are forced to make conciliation or, on the contrary, if there has, in fact, been a lack of love caused, perhaps unknowingly, by parental neglect, in which case the child truly is the victim of abandonment.

In the first case, we frequently find that the child feels no anxiety and no sense of abandonment when the reasons for the frustration have been explained (see Burlingham & Freud, 1942[22]), especially when explained by the adult with regret, which cannot be otherwise without the loving bond that joins them being damaged.

Subsequently, the child can accept the explanation or reject it by way of revolt. In either event, the problems that created and beset with difficulties such a life are solely to blame, not the parents and not the child. Consequently, the problem becomes one of adapting to reality, and not a question of affective security.

In contrast, the privations of love arising from non-objectively justified origins, such as in the innumerable instances of *false maternal presence*, are faced by the infant in isolation with no understanding of the consequential anxiety that is experienced. The distancing is felt as the incomprehensible trough widens. However, because the truth is so elusive, even the most caring of mothers can usually only provide false or superficial explanations—which are recognised as such by the child—for these grave disturbances. Analysis has shown that it is essential for the subject to have a proper understanding of the actual causes that resulted in his or her profound infantile torment. Following abandonic tendency, which, as we know, is dominated by self-depreciation in all situations and circumstances, initial patient responses will express inferiority: "I am not worthy of being loved" and culpability: "and it's my own fault because I'm bad".

Through direct observations of children, we can pose questions that connect, first, the fact of being loved to, second, feelings of per-sonal value. This is an issue of primary importance and about which we have gathered specific evidence. Generally, as already indicated (Chapter One, p. 20), there exists a causal relationship between the two because real love is solely responsible for feelings of self-worth.

Fenichel, in his most recent work, which is a type of "analytic summary", puts it in these terms: "The infant loses self-esteem when love is lost, self-esteem is found again with the rediscovery of love" (1945, p. 41).

And again,

> This fear of losing love is more intense than if it only represented a rational judgment in the face of real danger. This is because first and foremost self-esteem depends on exterior inputs, so the loss of such care and protection also means the loss of self-esteem. An ego that is loved feels strong, an abandoned ego is enfeebled and feels exposed to danger. (Fenichel, 1945, p. 43)

Fenichel's assertions on infant psychology warrant some attention here because they characterise a certain view that, in my opinion, is too broadly held within the analytic community. Specifically, a lot of analytic research seems to be based on observations of infant affective and instinctual reactions, but which totally leave aside the problem that surrounds the different stages of childhood intellectual development. So that when the word "ego" is used in this research, it is without any precise reference to levels of structural advancement and stages of development that is implied by the term. So I am a little surprised to see that from beneath the erudite pen of a practitioner such as Fenichel, with his great wealth of experience, comes affirmation both so absolute and with so little intellectual justification, which completely ignores all we know regarding the development of thought and judgement in the infant. Fenichel does ratify the common sense view, held by many parents and teachers, that there is some relationship between a child normatively surrounded by a loving environment and acquired feelings of personal value. However, he provides no explanation for these facts and the problems they raise are neither discussed nor even listed. Thus, reading *The Psychoanalytic Theory of Neurosis* leaves an impression that this category of problem, precisely because it is never mentioned, is of no interest to the analyst. I cannot agree with this viewpoint. The child is a whole entity and if our knowledge of thought formation does not sufficiently inform our understanding of affect and impulse, then grasping any comprehension of emotional and instinctual evolution, which is to say, examining it contextually within the framework that instigates the stages of thought development and judgement in the child, seems to me an impossibility.

In my opinion, Fenichel's position imposes a view that is too general, particularly concerning the progressive acquisition of inner self-value. This issue is of paramount importance in both general psychology, to enable more effective teaching, and in psychopathology, by clarifying the genesis of not only abandonment neurosis, but other neuroses also, notably those centred on issues of inferiority and authority.

To gain an understanding of this issue we can distinguish, in the child, the following acquisitions.

- Feelings of security where an ego is loved, so feels strong, as opposed to an ego that has been abandoned, so feels enfeebled and senses exposure to danger.
- Feelings of self-confidence, more or less conscious, which in the infant are a simple echo of trust in the confidence shown by the adult.
- Feelings of self-esteem that have begun to involve judgement formation, which initially is probably copied from the adult, but goes on to become increasingly autonomous.
- Feelings of self-worth based on accurate assessments of personal value, free of any borrowings and demonstrating genuinely independent thought and emotion.

It appears, then, that feelings of personal value are acquired step-by-step in a process that spans several tiers. Under so-called normal conditions, at what age does a child take these steps, by what process, and what exactly are the factors that help or hinder the journey? As yet, these are questions that we cannot answer, which is to say, our current understanding of this issue makes it impossible to know, with any empirical precision, the full extent and influence that love has in the evolution of an individual's sense of self-value. The question is complex and must not be presented, as it often is, simplistically. However, what does appear certain is that the ongoing presence of love and solicitude are the indispensable foundations upon which feelings and an overall sense of security is built.

Of those who were not endowed with this sense of security during early childhood, it seems few are able to go on to acquire significant feelings of self-confidence and personal value. Yet, for those few fortunate individuals who do, a particularly supple affectivity is developed which provides exceptional psychological equilibrium. Others, however, particularly those previously described with a predisposed vulnerability, remain fixed to the frustrations from this primary period of their lives and can find no sense of self.

Returning from this necessary digression to the role played by the familial component in abandonment neurosis, we can affirm that the parents' emotional attitude towards their children is of great importance in either arousing anxiety and insecurity or in its prevention. By affective attitude, we mean, on the one hand, the parents' feelings and the subsequent behaviour it prompts towards their child and, on the other, their manifest sense of responsibility directed towards every aspect of life, people, and objects generally. Insecurity is born of parents who are devoid of affection or hardened, but even in cases where parents are loving and understanding, but also anxious themselves, then, unwittingly, they will create a climate of anxiety. Either environment will manufacture fear in the child and feelings of imminent catastrophe. This kind of influence is particularly evident in the anxious baby, whose manic state is aggravated by the absence of love and understanding, or the lack of psychological balance in the parents. Alternatively, when parents do fulfil their duty of care, they exercise a reassuring and curative action, which, in some cases, will protect the child from neurosis.

We shall now move on to consider the third primary cause of abandonment neurosis, *abandonment trauma*. Those abandonics already referred to, stricken as a result of endogenous causes and who have always been chronic sufferers from insecurity and anxiety, are the most frequently occurring. For these subjects, analysis highlights a number of small but painful events, which the patient feels as a relentless source of injury and frustration that has been woven into the fabric of life. It is a predispositional state, exacerbated by the addition of defective familial dynamics sparking chronic anxiety which all combine, working slowly to penetrate and install the neurosis.

The alternative case, seemingly less frequent but more striking, must also be examined here. This is where an act, or acts, of actual abandonment has predominance in the patient's history, and manifestly marked a turning point in psychical development.

I am not certain if a material act of abandonment alone can result in neurotic trauma. However, we need to bear in mind that there is never an occurrence of trauma from such an event in an exceptionally healthy subject. Nevertheless, I pose the following question: can the trauma from a real abandonment ever be the essential cause in the development of an abandonment neurosis? Some cases seem to indicate that this can occur, but they are rare and require the combination of circumstances that are quite exceptional.

Example 19: Three children were living in the peaceful ambience that existed between their father and mother, when the latter, no doubt in a state of crisis, suddenly found great enthusiasm for another man, and no less abruptly abandoned the matrimonial home. Of the three abandoned children, the two older daughters, although suffering chagrin, did so normally, the youngest alone, a son, sank into the shadow of abandonment anxiety.

This, it seems, is indeed an example of trauma inducing the neurosis, with the child having no previous history of the condition. Must we conclude, then, that trauma, caused by the mother's abandonment of the child, shattered a positive and persistent oedipal bond in the eight-year-old boy who remained in great need of maternal solicitude? Or, without being previously apparent, could the child have been carrying a latent tendency towards anxiety? Either way, we cannot be certain, but it is likely that, in this case, the contrast between the secure state that preceded the trauma, then the feelings of betrayal that arose as a result of such a sudden and unexpected abandonment, at a very delicate age, suffices to explain the neurotic onset in the absence of predispositional particulars.

So, it would appear that certain cases of abandonment can hit with no warning—to the child, at least—as a total bolt out of the blue with an impact that is catastrophic, but it seems, however, that they are few and far between.

Mostly, we find that patients have a pre-history of the trauma. Although not consciously aware of the fact, their early life was often one of growing up amid a familial atmosphere that offered little security, or in which events could quickly degenerate into a state consistent with levels of dissatisfaction and latent anxiety. These are the initial traumas around which anxiety and the neurosis suddenly take shape and acquire all their virulence.

We see how the importance and the role of trauma are different depending on whether the trauma is catastrophic or catalytic. From the viewpoint of aetiology, in the former, frustration can be considered the principal catastrophic cause of the neurosis, which occurs only in exceptional cases. In most instances, the frustrating event is a catalytic trauma, which sets off a morbid infusion, a germination that grows and develops into the neurosis.

Psychoanalysts have now long recognised that the symptoms of abandonment anxiety, which, as a syndrome, I have sought to detail accurately and coherently here, generally have family fault as their primary cause: nurturing mistakes, and the lack of understanding and love on the part of parents.

Without wanting to minimise in any way the importance of this component, which I hope has been well enough identified here as the most decisive action in the formation of this neurosis, I would also like to highlight, at the risk of perhaps surprising some, the vital role that the constitutional, psycho-biological function also plays in the individual. The unconscious irresponsibility and ignorance of parents is so widespread as to appear impossible to combat. However, this is not the entire problem. I am speaking here to the newer generation of child analysts in particular, who are so often shocked by the extent of familial neglect they are confronted with. Yet, there are also many ordinary, normally attentive parents who suffer in attempting to care for their abandonic children, and to me it seems entirely inappropriate to judge their efforts detrimentally, given the enormity of this task. Abandonic mania is, by definition, anxiety that is limitless, and so insatiable. By definition also, the abandonic child can never be totally satisfied, regardless of the self-inflicted grief that might result in its pursuit. Only the adult who emerges, thanks to greater control, courtesy of an ego and intelligence able to rein in primitive impulse—but again, at what cost!—can reduce, limit, and contain this immeasurable appetite. It is left to the mothers and fathers, even—especially—those who are loving, to accomplish a task such as this that requires practically impossible levels of patience and perseverance.

This is why, it seems to me, it is honest and sensible of the analyst, when faced with adult abandonics, or the parents of abandonics, well some at least, to emphasise this crucial role, rather than the incurable constitutional factors that have an impact on the patient's character and behaviour.

Such remarks, regarding both therapeutic and pedagogic benefits, are not out of place here. Let me explain. I would stress that we should not, during the course of treatment, neglect or lose sight of any interwoven causes that could play a part in abandonment neurosis: whether the initial causes are bound to the patient's constitution, parental emotional attitude, abandonment trauma, or whether they are the result of second degree influences, by which I mean the creation and proliferation of symptoms one on top of the other, in the formation of a circular procession.

In any event, this kind of delicate approach to therapeutic work is the one most likely to be rewarded. We shall now move on to examine these methods in detail.

CHAPTER FOUR

Therapy

Guidelines for prognosis and analytic treatment

The more we advance the psychoanalytic method, the more we realise the need to clearly distinguish between patients whose symptoms are, and are not, likely to be either cured or relieved as a result of analysis. Too often, analytic treatment is considered a universal panacea. This is a belief that remains prominent among analysts themselves, despite the many failures that may otherwise have been foreseen. Treatment that is both long and costly for patient and analyst should not, in my view, be undertaken without the establishment of a precise diagnosis and an appropriately accurate prognosis.

In this regard, according to my experience, there are three indicators that will show how well the abandonic will respond to treatment: the intensity and character of the *masochism*, the intensity and character of the *aggression*, and the ability to *love*, in terms of minimum reciprocal capacity.

A current problem we have with the first indicator, *masochism*, is that it raises many questions that psychoanalysts and biologists are still not able to answer, so it would be inappropriate to raise them here. Even if we admit the "destructive tendency" and the "death instinct", as Freud hypothesised, the factual domain does not provide anything new for the analyst, so the area remains problematic. Even after so many years of analytic practice, we are often confounded by the violence of impulses that appear as anti-evolutionary and which we have assembled beneath the name "primary masochism", thanks to the astounding perspicacity with which Freud revealed observations as unexpected as they are seemingly incontestable.

We have looked at the central role *masochism* plays in abandonment neurosis and its many nuances. In certain patients, we recognise from the outset that masochism is the primary reaction and that, in contrast to its self-destructive tendencies, the analysis offers a taste of life, an ability to savour its joys, and a resilience of character that bodes well for treatment. In other patients, on the contrary, it seems all dynamism has been destroyed and the taste of pleasure or joy is non-existent. Here, the masochism appears to be constitutional, which seems nonsense from a biological viewpoint, so explains nothing, but does signify the state of things to be reckoned with. It becomes, then, a matter of intuition and practice to monitor whether or not the intensity and apparent constitutional character of this masochism allows hope of amelioration.

Even though *aggression* does not pose the same kind of biological and philosophical problems as *masochism*, from a practical point of view it must, none the less, be examined in the same way. Which is to say that we gauge intensity levels in each case, and establish if the aggression is essentially reactive or constitutional. Negative findings on these two points are a less definitive contraindication for analytic treatment than a conclusion verifying strong constitutional masochism. However, faced with a patient whose nature is seemingly bound to high levels of aggression, in order to achieve a positive outcome it is essential to ensure the existence of the collaborative analytic elements: intelligence, clarity of mind, desire for healing, absence of an overly cumbersome narcissism, etc.

The third point of consideration, which is no less important, I have termed the patient's ability to *love*. As with intelligence endowment and activity potential, it would seem certain that the ability to *love* varies from one individual to another. If these variations in emotional mode and intensity are yet to be measured precisely in some advanced psychological study, none the less they constitute a reality that is of paramount importance for analysts. In this instance, the difficulty resides in bringing the analysand's latent possibilities to fruition, in place of the oppressive compliance with his or her present reality.

Given that the patient is presenting with an abandonment neurosis, this permits the *a priori* supposition that he or she is afflicted by certain high intensity feelings. However, we still need to know the characteristics of that affectivity because, during the course of analysis, the abandonic can come to turn the page on the past and to accept what has been, while simultaneously renouncing present claims for reparation in favour of constructive activity, which are the realisation of those latent interior possibilities such as understanding and generosity. Without the development of these reciprocal capacities, narcissism will persist. Males will stay calculating and acutely egocentric, and females will remain miserly, demonstrating in all circumstances very little evidence of generosity. Such cases are problematic analytically.

Conclusions on a subject's suitability for treatment are based directly on observations of these three essential components: *masochism*, *aggression*, and the ability to *love*. On deciding to proceed, the prognosis and treatment duration can be roughly set. The negative-repulsive is typically treated over a longer period and has a less favourable prognosis than the positive-attractive. With naturally lower levels of masochism and aggression, the positive-attractive abandonic is, for the most part, better placed because of the ability to love. In contrast, the negative-repulsive faces developmental problems that are, inevitably, far more numerous and difficult to overcome because of emotional frugality imposed both on the self and others.

Technique

Ego analysis and the active technique

The symptomatology of abandonment neurosis reveals that the crux of abandonic conflict resides not in the unconscious, but in the ego. Here, pathological reaction is grouped around two centres that are of direct concern to the ego: the capacity to love, including its preferred method, and forms of defence.

After gathering an initial general impression of the patient's orientation, the analyst then needs to guide the subject, not by prompting a continued recounting of neurotic history, but, rather, with interventions that encourage the exploration of current experience and accessible, everyday detail. This material is used to push the abandonic relentlessly towards analysing the two erroneous focal points of this neurosis: the insatiable need for love, and the fear that drives resistance. This analytic strategy has a double objective.

The first is to provide for abandonics a clear awareness of their infirmity and a precise understanding of their characteristic pathological reactions, because, even in cases of extreme and conscious emotional rapacity (cf. Chapter One, p. 3), we can be more or less assured that the patients have not acquired a factual assessment of their actual condition, and that on every incriminating occasion, from the first to the last, the external world will immediately be held to account as the sole entity responsible for their failures and suffering.

The second is for the analyst to place value on the habitually normative elements of patient behaviour, which will gradually empower the abandonic, thereby also instilling a sense of responsibility. Regarding the secondary aetiology, it is imperative continuously to monitor the subject's personal sense of non-value and its development within the neurosis. Also, throughout the analysis, it is necessary to carefully calculate the ego's resistance strength before providing the analysand with interpretations that are difficult to accept.

In certain cases, it is necessary to begin the analysis, or perhaps I should say precede it, with a curative enriching of the patient's ego, either because it is virtually non-existent or because it is debilitated to the point of having no self-supporting capacity (cf. Chapter One, Example 9, p. 21).[23] Otherwise, lacking any clear feelings of value and security, the patient can face neither painful present events nor past traumas. This is a state of being that can spark inhibition at the outset of treatment and, as anxiety grows, can bar any incidence of ecphory,[24] as it occurs in the treatment of other neuroses, as well as rendering the analysand almost completely mute. This is not only unhelpful and unnecessary, but has the added effect of initiating a depressive episode that becomes increasingly passive. Here again, it is crucial that the analyst intervene, explain the intolerable psychic traumas of the past, and fortify the ego by highlighting its positive qualities. During the course of analysis, prior to particularly painful evocations, it might be necessary to utilise the same technique, thereby avoiding profoundly sterile and destructive blockages in the analysand generated by extreme feelings of worthlessness. However, it needs to be emphasised that this technique must not be used without all due consideration, and neither should it be applied with feelings of compassion on the part of the analyst, who has to be mindful that this kind of ego support must be only temporary, and measured closely against the analysand's progress with the aim of moving on post-haste.

From the outset of treatment, there needs to be a careful analysis of current experience. Even material relating to the subject's history should be viewed in the light of present life circumstance and detail, in order to constantly highlight the links between abandonic reaction to past events, frustrating individuals in particular, and current responses within present relationships. As I have already said, the abandonic confronts us with a neurosis that is extremely active and has been neither repressed nor accepted, and, in most cases, the subject will recount his or her experiences *ad infinitum*. The analyst must, therefore, avoid allowing abandonics—here again, contrary to standard treatment in most other neuroses where the analysand evokes into consciousness many painful, previously repressed memories—to become bogged down in their unproductive *rumination* on the past. This development can become increasingly exacerbated if analysands are simply given free rein to bemoan what could be termed their well-worn affects. It is a chronic, dull, and lifeless pain, a lament that displaces true emotion.

Conversely, if the analyst actively demonstrates that knowledge of the patient's past is of no interest except in terms of how it can affect and modify life in the present, the analysand, jolted from the tired habit of sterile complaint, becomes agitated and will often revolt, fearing the analyst has stolen the indispensable source of grievance that feeds the analysand's masochism. However, gradually, the subject comes to see, and especially feel, everything regarding his or her past life in a new way. Thus, emotion is mobilised, permitting its effective discharge, and drawing into consciousness the actual events or situations that were truly traumatic.

Transference and utilisation of the new analytic relationship

All neuroses cause alterations to familial and social exchange; with abandonment anxiety, we find problematic relations are not only situated at the point of neurotic genesis, but that they remain a central component.

In my experience, if analysts limit themselves to classical forms of treatment, offering reasons for the analysand's failures on a purely theoretical level while remaining strictly impersonal, those interpretations are ineffective. It seems the analysand, who, in childhood, never knew the experience of security in a human relationship, on the one hand has difficulty grasping what is expected and, on the other, as an adult, no longer has sufficient affectivity to risk further investment.

This observation has caused me to reflect on the extremely complex analytic relationship that exists within the therapeutic setting, and on the components that may be drawn from it in the treatment of abandonment neurosis.

It seems to me that Freud's discovery of transference mechanisms and their essential function in treatment has caused some analysts to lose sight of other elements that make up the analytic relationship. I am speaking here of diverse reactions and feelings which are neither repetitions nor parts of the transference from past experiences or objects, but, rather, very much to the contrary, which constitute a brand new experience for the analysand because the situation is also absolutely new. Here, the subject discovers the experience of being heard and understood in the absence of judgemental criticism, and the opportunity to say and express all without provoking any aggressive reactions or abandonment by the analyst, whose attitude and behaviour can be completely relied upon in terms of consistency, equality, and objectivity, etc. In the more classical analytic setting also, where the rule of maximum impartiality is applied by the analyst, we cannot deny that this therapeutic investigation is likewise based on equality, patience, and perseverance, those revered elements of human behaviour never before encountered by most neurotics. It would seem, then, that the action of these highly valued components in analysis plays a part of equal importance to that of transference. This is a complex role that, rather than being ignored, needs to be studied and clarified.[25]

An even more compelling reason, when working with abandonics, to utilise the active technique being advocated here is that these valued elements have a greater propensity to emerge. The "active" analyst becomes, by necessity, less impersonal and, therefore, better "known" to the analysand, despite still enforcing with absolute rigour—which in my view remains essential—the rule of never allowing any part of personal or private life to contaminate the analysis. In the eyes of the analysand, it also seems to generate a much greater appreciation of the painstaking work being carried out on his or her behalf by the analyst, effort that can easily go unnoticed in a subject who is demonstrably, or even subtly, passive, the fact of which the analysand is often unaware.

This tireless, comprehensive effort, free from rebuke, generally becomes lauded by the analysand as something beyond monetary worth because its value and exceptional qualities are never diminished, despite having to pay the analyst.

In the treatment of abandonment neurosis, these findings have led me to exploit the analytic relationship in a more thorough manner than can be applied using classical technique, and this can be seen from dual points of view. First, because it reveals to the analyst, then—courtesy of the interpretations—to the analysand, the inappropriate behaviours apparent in the subject's everyday life. Second, by revealing to the analysand a new quality of relationship based on stability, good will, trust, and, very gradually, reciprocity.

The examples listed below will provide a better grasp of how best to utilise this kind of analytic relationship. Initially, it might seem as if the technique moves exactly along classical lines, as interpretations of the transference lead the analysand to become conscious of their repetitive self-sabotage. However, the abandonic, who has never experienced a relationship that could be considered normal, will constantly refer to past mistakes, so is not limited only to those that become manifest in the transference. Being placed in a new relationship will elicit new nefarious behaviour, which is full of latent consequences, and, as such, becomes available to the analysis. Once the analysand–analyst relationship starts operating on a level that is more active and more humane, the potential for erroneous conduct is broadened. This allows the patient's affectivity and method of social interaction to be more accurately scrutinised, at a time when he or she is still unable to establish normative relationships. Also, to forewarn about potential neurotic reaction is to forearm the analysand, which will encourage the risking of affective involvement outside of the analysis sooner rather than later.

Examples

The problem of interruptions to analysis, holiday breaks, sickness, etc.

For the abandonic, interruptions to the regular sessions and regime of analytic treatment have a much greater impact than they do on the other neurotic types. These breaks symbolise abandonment, immediately triggering anxiety and a return by the analysand to characteristic modes of defence, with displays of aggression, isolation, reactive masochism, etc. During the course of analysis, these interruptions can serve, if the patient is truly motivated rather than the subject of self-deception, as an indicator to the analyst of both the progress that has been made by the analysand and as a means of encouraging in the subject an attitude that is less possessive and self-centred. The benefits this reality test offers are acquired precisely through ensuring these interruptions have no artificial characteristics. So, first, the maximum possible amount of prior warning must be given, at the beginning of analysis anyway, so that the analysand is not taken by surprise and time can be taken in the following sessions to explore all manifest reactions. Second, the analyst must not fear or hesitate to frankly declare his or her motives: the need for rest or for personal work, etc., to impress upon the patient the reasons why this effort is required. But as with a child—and is this not the case?—it is essential to push slowly, "allowing" the analyst, in this instance, to generate a shifting of attitude from captive aggression to amiable generosity. The work should be slow, and assessed in the most thorough way possible in order to avoid, on the one hand, in the positive-attractive "spoilt child", a lingering desire for vindication that can become dominant and, on the other, in the negative-repulsive, the need over months of treatment and in all other situations and settings to get rid of the rancour which is felt as a constant pressure.

The abandonic, by definition, is horrified at the prospect of having to share. Jealousies are frequently encountered here aimed at other analysands. These reactions are generally, but not always, a consequence of the transference. In some cases, where this problem is particularly grave, past a certain point into the analysis when I am confident that a sufficient level of ego strength has been acquired, I put the analysand to the test. Here again, there must be no contrivance. On the contrary, we can profit from a busy period in the practice where there are not enough analytic hours in the day, and ask analysands if he or she would be willing to sacrifice one of theirs in favour of another patient who has a greater need. Such a strategy has the double advantage of bolstering feelings of worth in the abandonic, who will feel at a more advanced stage of healing than the other patient, while at the same time enabling him or her to experience a greater sense of confidence in the analyst. Either way, success or failure is a boost to the analysis, extracting strongly affective material from what is being experienced in the present.

The problem of gifts

A strictly classical approach prohibits the acceptance of any gift from patient to analyst. This is, in my view, a rule that is too general and absolute in its attempt to resolve an issue that is multi-faceted. Gifts are offered by patients as expressions of guilt, narcissism, substitution, where the gift is a pledge of greater effort, or inferiority, where the gift represents a belief that the subject has nothing else to offer, or as symbols of aggression. These offerings and the many others that all serve an unconscious function for the analysand can be indispensable to the analysis, along with those gifts that are given as a conscious expression of true feeling. In any event, regardless of cost or its absence, I am of the view that these offerings need to be examined in the context of the whole analytic experience, in terms of transference and the creation of what is, for the abandonic, a new and unprecedented type of relationship. To refuse all gifts, it seems, is to sidestep what are perceived as potential problems and, in fact, deny the analysis valuable discoveries that can be extracted from these objects.[26]

The problem of analyst infallibility

Abandonment neurosis could also be called the neurosis absolute. The problem of analyst infallibility, where the analysand sees the therapist as physically and psychically flawless, is felt with greater acuity by the abandonic than in the other forms of neurosis. Abandonics are also more susceptible to inundation by profound levels of anxiety than the other neurotic types if their thirst for the absolute or their total need for security is at all shaken in their connection to the analyst. It is important to test and closely monitor whether the subject's view of both physical and psychical reality is progressing into ever-sharper focus, which can be measured according to the capacity for resistance and the developmental stage that has been reached. Advancement here is a coup for probity, where the analysand adapts to the real by accepting his or her relationship with it, while abolishing previously held fears.[27] The female analyst who is frail in appearance and health will be compensated both by lower levels of subject resistance, and the subsequent analytic material that will flow as a result.

The attachment objection

This objection is not exclusive to patients, but also exists among analysts, where the fear is that an analysand will continue to cling, remaining fixed to a dependency on the analyst. When presenting to colleagues my theory of the active technique as applied in the treatment of abandonics, the objection of interminable attachment to the analyst is often raised.

My experience is the opposite. Reviewing my case histories for this publication, I could find only one instance of such ongoing dependency. The abandonic in question was a lesbian, in whom I could not instil an objective disposition and sense of liberation, but this analysis dates back eleven years, to a time when my understanding of abandonment anxiety was still quite vague, so the therapy also lacked focus and, I must confess, when faced by the intricate complexity of her dilemmas, all built on problematic constitutional foundations, the only treatment I could offer might have been erroneous.

Since then, over the last five to six years in particular, by which time the technique revealed within these pages had been developed in detailed precision, I have never encountered a case of ongoing attachment dependency, either in male or female patients. The reasons seem to be twofold:

1. The complete eradication of anxiety as far as is possible. We know at what point fear of losing his or her object, with all the ambivalence this position implies, fixes the abandonic as subject. This is the first pitfall to avoid. If the healing crisis (see below, p. 92) is wrongly interpreted and badly administered, or if the end of analysis is not elaborated with all technical care, anxiety and attachment to the analyst will persist. An ego that remains feeble will sabotage the redeployment of its energies and

continue in its previous function of regressing back to maternal fixation. If, in contrast, the analysand is closely monitored for every possible occasion that may arise that serves to regenerate the anxiety, and if the abandonic's resistance in facing reality's hardships has been sufficiently demonstrated to him or her, a sense of security will be acquired that allows the subject to separate from the analyst with ease.

2.   A careful distinction needs to be made that separates the transference, either positive or negative, from the new and valued attachment, in order to eliminate the former and enrich the latter. This enrichment of normative feelings experienced by the analysand *vis-à-vis* the analyst also needs to be handled with care. I shall pause here briefly and emphasise the critical nature of this point, because, in my view, its importance is often underestimated by analysts who might be inclined to overvalue the transference at the expense of recognising objectively motivated sentiments made by the analysand, which is, without doubt, so that the analyst can avoid facing the difficulties the expression of these feelings raise.

The primary indication that an analysand has acquired normative feelings of self-value is when the analyst no longer harbours any concern that the patient might still be under threat from the negative forces of his or her own affectivity. It is important here to provide a full appreciation of what are, for the analysand, most often very new feelings. It is also appropriate that the analyst talk with a shared respect of this emotional acquisition, or what are, for the subject, newly discovered riches. If these feelings are of affection, gratitude, and confidence, conveyed with sensitivity, or even reciprocity through recognition of the analyst's ordeal in responding to the analysand with interest and solicitude, then the sentiments are authentic and genuinely motivated.[28] However, if these become feelings of love and erotic desire, the analyst must speak with the same calm respect, explaining to the analysand that in analysis, as in life, reality throws up obstacles in one situation or another, where the primary objective is not always the pursuit of love. None the less, it is remarkable that this analysand can discover these feelings and desires towards someone held in such high esteem, which is often the first experience of its type without a subsequent disassociation, and find such satisfaction from normative attitudes and emotions that will surely prompt the search for another object who is worthy of this love and is free to return it. The fact of having found an initial love object is evidence for the analysand that others exist, and that there is potential for just such an attachment. In my experience, an understanding can be reached without undue difficulty where the analysand comes to accept that a loving attachment serves as a healing catalyst and that the privation of love, conversely, can result in a form of interior death, so if periodic suffering is caused in the search for love, then this ordeal is a means which ultimately justifies a very valuable end.

The proper appreciation and orientation of this new affectivity evident in the analysand, it seems to me, depends primarily on the deep personal convictions and attitudes, both conscious and unconscious, of the analyst, as demonstrated through intelligence, the total absence of fear, simplicity, truth, and absolute human respect.

This is to say that the analyst's personality and equilibrium in maintaining a rigorous analytic methodology—an issue, it seems, that is often left in the shadows for fear of the problems it may raise—does in fact play, in my view, an extremely important role.

The healing crisis

The onset of healing is one of the most critical phases, if not *the* most critical phase, in the course of an abandonic analysis. If the significance of this phase goes unrecognised, or if the analyst does not respond adequately to the new disturbances produced, all the work accomplished to this point will be compromised and the abandonic will be plunged into depression.

This crisis occurs when the patient is on the cusp of adapting to the real, which is to say, renouncing the need for vengeance and compensation for the past, renouncing previous forms of love or other infantile demands, and renouncing the desire for the absolute. Such renunciation represents, for the analysand, the shift towards a life that consists of more than sacrifice. However, the effort is so great that, on the verge of surrender, the entire neurosis stiffens resolve. Up to this point, the abandonic had a precise reason for living, which consisted of intense affect charging a quest for revenge, compensation for past injustice, and satisfying an infantile need to be loved, where the ego's sole objective was to facilitate the playing out of these captive tendencies.

The purging of this very fluid neurosis necessarily results in profound disarray, where, for the abandonic, everything suffers from a kind of "disaffection", and nothing holds attraction, flavour, or meaning. The *raison d'être* having been lost, a dark depression descends.

Example 20: The letter of an abandonic amid the healing crisis: "More tears, more rebellion, and defence in the face of my life's suffering. Resignation. No more dynamism, no impetus, no feeling, no hope, just the conviction of a life irredeemably lost. All is worthless. I have always thought everything would resolve, that belief is now bankrupt. Dead. This resignation is horrific, and the prospect of renunciation makes me want to curl into a ball. I mourn no longer being an abandonite[29] for the dynamism that has been lost."

Example 21: And another: "This despair without substance, what good can it serve in the face of all, partnered with the sense of a much more ordered self, with greater clarity, and a general demeanour so much better adapted to normal life, but without purpose."

Often the analysand, at this point in treatment, suddenly complains of feeling old, worn out, and powerless. Consciously relinquishing the greater part of infantile and childhood characteristics, the analysand quickly assumes his or her actual age.

Example 22: Mrs I, after a series of sessions on the necessity for her to renounce a desire of the absolute, said, "I feel old, the days, the weeks pass, and feel like centuries crushing down."

Example 23: Mr P, "As I have changed, so my youth has evaporated. I feel twenty more years has drained from me."

The analysand mourns the death of a self that hitherto has been known, loved, and whose illusions are now lost. "Better to suffer for having lost the absolute, rather than accept the loss", a patient once said to me, "to suffer is to retain the past."

During the crisis, all therapeutic problems can be very painful for the analysand and critical for the analyst, who must push the patient towards a redeployment of energies, which, up until this point "arranged everything" in terms of the need for vengeance or reparation of the past. This redeployment is difficult. Adult satisfactions, which must displace infantile pleasures, are scant, not having been sufficiently experienced. In speaking of prompting this redeployment towards a new dynamism, I do not mean by way of the analyst knowing all and giving practical advice. For, in spite of sometimes wanting to do just this, we are assured, as Freud demonstrated, that any such attempt is futile and would itself represent one more obstacle to recovery from this neurosis. What I do mean is for the analyst to clear the way for aspiration, enabling the patient to dare to look forward, and to confront and strive for what is wanted, if the fear can be overcome.

As the new developments are revealed to the analysand, so the analyst must ensure that every mechanism of avoidance that threatens the patient is closely monitored, and that strong support is provided regarding the patient's adaptive efforts towards the real. All mechanisms of the crisis must be explained so that, rather than a regression, it is a crisis of growth.

Technique for the termination of analysis

Just as ignorance of the healing crisis can derail an analysis and leave the patient to languish in a worsened condition, it is equally the case that too much care cannot be taken in the termination of an abandonic analysis. This end, however, must not follow too closely on the heels of the healing crisis.

Here, broad-ranging flexibility is needed in order to cater for the peculiarities of the abandonic patient in question. Experience shows, for example, that an abrupt end, however well analysed and planned in advance according to conventional technique, is inapplicable in the termination of an abandonic analysis because it does not prevent relapse.

It must be remembered, and it needs to be impressed upon the analysand, that he or she will remain, to a greater or lesser extent, vulnerable to the frustrations of life and the predisposition of anxiety, and that what the analysis has provided is a personal interior security, in addition to a method for generating and maintaining this security in the face of threat, a security we gradually lead the abandonic to be assured of without the analyst's assistance.

For a period of time that must be decided and assessed according to each individual case, sessions need to be regularly terminated with the abandonic having been set certain "goals", which is to say, with review dates that are fixed in advance where the analyst will share an assessment of progress with the analysand. Here, it is possible to apply a diverse range of techniques, the simplest being to place intervals of up to one, two, or even three months between these sessions. Cases where progress is solid need less intervention, but care must be taken not to set dates too far in advance, so a modicum of control is maintained. Remember never to leave the analysand without something precise and substantial to focus on before he or she is capable of self-support.

With some patients, who need to make a concerted push towards autonomy, experience has taught me not to hesitate in taking the initiative from time to time to question them, which is a mark of interest not so much to do with reassurance as to demonstrate one final time that relationships can be stable and faithful. Once again, a complete difference will be observed here between classical analytic technique and that which, in my view, is indispensable to the treatment of abandonment neurosis. Up until the very termination of analysis, it is essential never to lose sight of the analyst's responsibility to give the analysand the new knowledge of this new type of quality relationship.

For this technique to bear fruit at the end of analysis, progressively liberating the analysand from his or her obsession with *external* relations by providing a truly autonomous and emotionally secure *internal* sense of self, every aid and example must be deployed gradually over the last months of treatment to show the patient the absolute necessity for each human being to *internalise affective relationships*. Below is an outline of the technique I have subsequently developed. It is essential to give the analysand minimal explanations of the following psychological phenomena:

The emotional and intellectual reality of the infant, which resulted in a confusion with such profound consequences for our subject, was caused by the qualitative and quantitative absence or suppression—in effect, loss—of externally manifest feelings from others: proof of love, for example, in both act and intent, etc.

The concept of human development, in terms of becoming an adult with the ability to abstract, was not hitherto grasped in any concrete fashion.

As a result, evolution from abstraction to internalisation did not occur, internalisation being the mechanism that permits continuous possession even in absence, so is able to maintain a belief, credited to the love object, without the constant need for proof.

Based on these three fundamental principles, the analyst needs to stress that there is a basic requirement for thought in all affective relationships, in order to make well motivated choices and understand the meaning and value of any particular liaison. The result will be thoughtful relationships, which can be partially independent of their own exterior manifestations—internalised, in other words—with contingencies that supply a new security, motivated from within rather than externally, so with prospects infinitely more continuous and stable.

In my experience, even newly evolving abandonics are able to capture precisely these explanations, provided the analyst expresses them clearly and is not afraid to call upon multiple examples.

Some specific technical problems

The interrelation between infantile modes of thought and neurotic behaviour

Ordinarily, analysis seeks essentially to enlighten the analysand about the instinctual and affective mobility of his or her neurosis. The technique highlighted in the previous paragraph is certainly useful in this respect, but becomes especially so in the treatment of pre-Oedipal neuroses, where evidence of neurotic thought in its various modes is also revealed with no less care.

Anachronistic intellectual mechanisms, coupled with strong infant fixations, constitute for the ego powerful neurotic symptoms as harmful as those that impact on instinctive and emotional life.

Moreover, it should not be forgotten that these anachronistic modes of thought are the moulds into which this neurosis flows or, to put it another way, they are the tools it exploits. Making analysands conscious of these judgemental errors and the infantile inferences upon which their reasoning rests, while at the same time revealing the use their neurosis has made of these ill-conceived thoughts, liberates analysands' egos from those shackles and single-handedly facilitates the growth towards adulthood.

I shall not dwell further on this problematic process, which in itself is a subject that could fill another book, save to say the analysand needs to be made fully aware of the central role it plays in abandonment neurosis, with particular regard to: *magical thought* (cf. Frazer, Lévy-Bruhl, Piaget, etc.), *intellectual realism*, in the sense that Piaget, follow-ing Luquet, employs the term (Piaget, 1930).

These two factors are evident and active in the difficulty the abandonic has in distinguishing *the ego from the non-ego*, in terms of projection, introjection and identification; *the internal from the external*, where there is a rejection of exterior reality through displacement by projected subjectivity, and the rejection of responsibility for any-thing externally derived, especially in the frequent case where there is a personification of neurotic symptoms, so that the subject has "become" the animal, the other, the particular character etc.; the ficti-tious from the real; the subjective from the objective.

These intellectual anachronisms and the impediments they consti-tute with regard to the progression towards adult thought are always the result, except in cases of mental abnormality, of arrested emotional development. The causal objective is to acknowledge the neurotic need to remain fixed at this stage of infancy, where the subject does not learn normative thought, but instead obeys pre-logical infantile laws, in the psychic realms, at least, where the neurosis is rife.

Conversely, it is this absence of clear thought, with its reliance on principles of non-contradiction and the rules of logic and objectivity, which maintains the neurosis in its affective confusion. There is, how-ever, action and reaction between these two domains, where impact on a range of significant factors in one, by necessity, affects the other, so there is simultaneous intervention occurring in both, which quick-ens treatment by augmenting the analysand's awareness of self and the means of healing.

The mixed type

It is sometimes difficult at the beginning of an abandonic analysis to identify the particular stage of libidinal development the subject is thought to have attained. An important question to pose is: has the patient reached the stage of differentiation characterised by the Oedipus complex or not? Resolution of this issue is central to deter-mining an optimum form of treatment. There is often a problem here, however, in that the analyst can rarely rely on the data being supplied by the patient to facilitate accurate assessment. So, we must be on our guard and avoid making hasty judgements based on the analytic material the patient first brings, because, as a general rule, it is likely to be misleading on crucial points.

It is important to note that, in most cases where confusion persists in this regard, the analysis passes through three distinct phases:

First Phase: The subject unconsciously or deliberately camouflages his or her affective infantilism. Here, he or she will provide facts, memories, and dreams that seem to confirm a differentiation where individuals of the opposite sex do exist as such, and an oedipal orientation appears a good basis upon which to initially test object relations.

Second Phase: Behaviour and analytic material are subject to alteration. It seems the analysand, without realising it, removes the mask exposing the self, which is to say, the previous capacities are lost, leaving a child dogged by multiple fears and primitive types of attachment, where anxiety and abandonment neurosis appear in all of their specific manifestations.

Third Phase: Resurgence of oedipal material, but this time with a changed and sharply manifest affective hue, free of abandonment anxiety, characteristically differentiated with a courageous demeanour—masculine or feminine—so diametrically opposed to that of the first phase.

I have indicated elsewhere that there is a problem of interpretation raised by the progression of these three phases (Chapter Two, Part I, pp. 58–60). From the therapeutic perspective, we must, therefore, insist on the following points.

If, in the first phase, the analyst is caught in a trap of believing the pseudo-oedipal representation, and overestimating the patient's libidinal evolution, there is a danger of missing completely the profound infantile affectivity that is bound to abandonment anxiety.

The Oedipus complex, however crudely formed, marks a substantial step forward in the subject's development, and if its presence is wrongly assumed, then the analyst will be attempting to build on the vacuum of abandonment. The problematic crux having been overlooked, the analysis is rendered inoperable, being unable to reach the patient's deeper psychic structures.

To avoid this danger, the analyst must refrain from making oedipal interpretations until sufficient time has been provided to unmask the patient's most primitive affectivity by being vigilantly attuned to the detection of its existence, one which is all the more shameful in the analysand's eyes, given that the analysand considers himself or herself to be well adapted in certain areas of life and more intelligent than this conclusion would warrant.

Note: After writing the above, I was made aware of a remarkable article on the pre-oedipal stage, written by Mrs Lampl-de Groot.[30] In it, she emphasises the delicate clinical problem of how to distinguish the analysis of material that appears to be oedipal from that which is pre-oedipal. The difficulty of this distinction, she says, is due on the one hand to all stages of child development overlapping each other, and, on the other, because any given phase of development is always used, to a certain extent, to erase its predecessor.

One means of discerning the difference can be observed through the manner in which the material brought by the patient is communicated, with particular notice given to gestures and the attitudes that accompany them. Mrs Lampl-de Groot cites the example of a case provided by Mr Paul Federn, where, by way of illustration, he confirms striking observations I have observed in my own patients.

> A young man who had been through an analysis, and as a result of that work was to a large extent freed from inhibition, came to see me several years later suffering sexual dysfunction: impotence. Following some months of treatment, a comprehensive psychological history along with all the details of the first analysis, including the identification of an Oedipus complex, was revealed. However, the patient's behaviour then began to alter.
>
> During the initial stage of analysis he had communicated with ease in a strong clear voice, in spite of difficulties arising from the transference, when, for example, there was a revival of oedipal desires, plus his resistance taking a number of other forms. But as we moved into the second phase his personality changed completely. He no longer behaved as an adult, but began speaking as a child with incomplete phrases and a voice that became high pitched and infantile. His emotions and needs would fluctuate from one minute to the next. Sometimes he would cry like a baby lavishing love on me as his protector, then he would shout and externalise other intense manifestations of hostility. These ructions in the transference were snatches of

primitive fantasy, characteristic of the ambivalence we recognise as integral to infant emotional life. The content of these fantasies was totally passive: my role was to nurture, to nourish and to immediately satisfy his every need. But they were also intermingled with reactive eruptions, when the aggressive tendencies would manifest in an overflow of repressed anger and hatred crystallised through reproach and accusation. The slightest change in my vocal tone or movement in my chair became the starting point of attachment fantasies, or prompted outbursts of recrimination and explosive insult. These were amorous fantasies, expressing through both oral and anal tendency a desire to be caressed and pampered, the need for tenderness and the search for exhibitionistic satisfaction.

* * *

Also, while this acting out was taking place within the transference, outside the analysis the patient was occasionally manifesting similar behaviour patterns in his relationships with female partners. While primarily I represented the mother who, through identification with his father, he wanted to love but was not permitted to possess, at that time there was also an attempt to partially satisfy pre-Oedipal desires with a girl of lower social rank. Then, during the period which, in the transference, his early ambivalent mother attachment was revived, for a time he was in a relationship and came to adore a woman he knew who was significantly his senior, which coincided with the transference oscillating from one extreme to the other. But gradually, earlier events came into sharper focus: for example at the age of two he regularly sat on his mother's lap, was told stories and shown pictures. He related these experiences as feeling hot and delicious, speaking in the infantile way I have sought to characterise above. But he also remembered the hostility that rose from within when his mother refused to repeat or prolong these experiences that brought such indescribable joy. The memories of this period were scant. None the less the intensity and clarity of recognition in his analytic behaviour convinced us both of their veracity. Consequently, as an adult, he had a desire to create a family life, unconsciously searching for a woman who could replicate his pre-Oedipal mother, and provide in every detail a revival of these childhood experiences. However, the relationships that were able to satisfy these hostile and perverse traits became repugnant to parts of his adult personality. They blemished the adored image of the Oedipal mother, so it became impossible to reconcile love and sexuality, thereby prohibiting marriage and even sexual potency, despite his ego having approved the choice of partner. (Lampl-De Groot (1975)[1946], pp. 77 & 78)

I have recorded these observations verbatim because of their direct pertinence to the matter at hand. First, they provide evidence confirming the view I have outlined above suggesting that some analysts often display a tendency to overestimate the importance of an Oedipus complex, to the detriment of the pre-oedipal phase. In the case of Mr Federn's observations, we see this occurring in the first analysis, where central to the neurosis was a primitive—essentially passive and ambivalent—fixation to the mother, which was not dealt with and so remained intact. As a result, neurotic disturbances to emotional life persisted. Those were then eliminated by the second analysis, which, when complete, also had an ameliorating effect on the patient's professional life.

Second, the patient's behaviour in the face of both oedipal and pre-oedipal material testifies to the great difficulty and repugnance the analysand had dealing with the latter, while the former was accepted without any great disturbance.

Finally, it all testifies to the point I have been stressing: if the analysis is restricted to pseudo-oedipal material that is easily accessed in the first months of treatment, it prevents regression to the basic tenets of the patient's neurosis, that is to say, reliving and analysing the fixation of primary maternal attachment, which, in turn, impedes proper development of an Oedipus complex that most often becomes poorly differentiated as a result. So, structurally, the primacy of need is for security and not the genital sexuality that constitutes the state of development towards adulthood.

In fact, it is more a function of resistance that the pseudo-oedipal material is thrown up during the course of analysis. The subject stands sentry, guarding deeply rooted infantile fortifications, urging the analyst to direct treatment based on guilt derived from sexual rivalry and not, as should be the case, according to the enormous resistance generated by a narcissism dedicated to satisfying primitive need in the face of infantile terror and its ravages. It is precisely this intensely regressive material that the pseudo-oedipal ruse attempts to mask.

As the case cited by Mr Federn demonstrates, the acuity of opposition between childhood desire and adult need leaves the individual cruelly cleaved in the wake of contradictions created by such opposing impulses.

Symptoms subject to double interpretation

In the treatment of abandonment neurosis, the analyst can come across certain symptoms which may be interpreted in two different ways, depending on whether the prevailing point of view is strictly and classically Freudian or whether it follows the tenets of abandonment neurosis.

I spoke earlier of the diverse analytic data that subjects often supply where two subsequent interpretations are possible (see Chapter One, pp. 7 & 8). Here are some other examples.

Castration complex or abandonment anxiety?

Example 24: A young abandonic woman, newly married to a man with little sexual experience who suffered periodic impotence. Analysis revealed a marked hostility towards her husband's penis: "I do not like this machine", she would say.

Is this aggression towards men and the desire to castrate the result of penis envy, or is it a reaction in response to the frustration of love, synonymous with the lack of love and abandonment?

Theoretically, both hypotheses are founded. It is, none the less, consistently the former option that becomes the immediate choice of analysts schooled in the conventional mainstream. Practically speaking, however, this young woman did not present a castration complex and generally was well adjusted to a feminine disposition. In addition, her attitude, tone, and aggressive reaction to her husband's penis is typically the result of abandonment frustration.

In fact, the interpretation of abandonment anxiety produced palpable relief and gradually the young woman, having found affective security, was able to help her husband, contributing greatly to his restitution.

Castration complex or abandonment anxiety?

Example 25: Miss N lost her mother at age nine; she presented with a strong paternal fixation, which was interpreted by her first analyst in the oedipal sense. All the subsequent analytic material concerned the father and was seen as attached to this oedipal fixation, where conflicts with women, which the patient's history indicated were many, were viewed beneath the scope of rivalry for the father. After two years of analysis, some areas of this young woman's recovery were satisfactory. However, the foundations of her anxiety remained unchanged, which was precisely what brought her to me.

In this case, fixation to the father, it seemed to me, nullified differential oedipal material, or, at least, its presentation was sporadic and rare, masked and displaced by the search for maternal love. The father played a bisexual role, more feminine than masculine, whose function was essentially as a provider of security. Part of this conflict with other females was also attached to a search for the mother and the demands of an affectivity that remained excessively infantile.

Moreover, sexual non-differentiation pushed certain of these attachments increasingly towards erotic confrontations and misunderstandings implied by this latent homosexuality.

Oedipal triangle or a measure of security?

Example 26: Mr R, throughout youth, was attached only to married women; in the analysis he went through before coming to see me, this search for the triangular relationship was interpreted as a malformed, fluid Oedipus complex, which forced the replication and repetition of situations experienced in childhood. However, it was also the case that Mr R, as a small boy, knew no personal security, lived in fear of displeasing, being cowardly, and he was also outwardly passive and incapable of engaging with any of his real feelings.

As a result, later in life, he searched only to be desired and pampered, without ever having to take responsibility as a man for his chosen object. No feelings of rivalry ever arose in him towards the legitimate male partner. On the contrary, Mr R was happy to leave the husband charged with the virile function, a role that terrified the patient, knowing it was one he would be at pains to fulfil.

The patient had no more ability in the present than he had in the past to experience anything approaching a real Oedipus complex. Locked in passive fixation to the mother, with whom there was total identification, he sought, under the pretence of love, the recreation of this infantile relationship.

These examples—and there are many more—suffice to demonstrate that inappropriate psychoanalytic interpretations can often result when it is presumed that patients possess a level of ego and affective development which has in fact never been attained.

Conclusions

Danger of the classical method in the treatment of abandonment neurosis

Finally, analytic method is, in the view of many, the only therapeutic technique capable of providing the abandonic with maximum relief from profound anxiety, in addition to assurances of affective adaptation to the real. However, the successful application of this method is solely dependent upon the technical modifications I have endeavoured to clarify in the preceding pages.

Any honest and conscientious analyst would agree, I trust, that a failed analysis almost always results in a worsening of the patient's condition: better not to have experienced analysis than to suffer its failure. This general rule is always applicable in the case of abandonment neurosis, for reasons that are as understandable as they are apparent: the deeply disruptive consequence of a failed analysis relegates the abandonic to an even more acute disassociated state. The subject remains caught in the grip of unavowed primal fear, which sometimes was not even detected in the analysis, or, at least, was not revealed at its profound root cause. So, not only has the main objective of the analysis, adaption to the adult stage, failed, but the gap separating the abandonic from full maturity has actually widened. Furthermore, if the analysand is at least partially satisfied through not having been confronted with his or her profound infantilism, which he or she would prefer remain hidden, with the result that anxiety levels remain unchanged, as does the inability to love, to tolerate privations and separations, or to suffer this state of being, then feelings of justified ambivalence towards the analyst are nourished. The analyst, rather than having distilled a new, clear, true, happier, ambivalent free disposition, instead becomes, regardless of difficulties endured on the patient's behalf, an object of distrust and rancour. So, instead of providing a stepping-stone towards the realisation of love and attachment, the analyst is consigned to the ranks of those others who justify for the analysand feelings of bitterness and the desire for vindication. The abandonic, we know, is demanding and unforgiving. So, the analysis and the analyst must provide a refutation of these severe rules, and also allow the way to be opened for a new understanding and new judgements. If the analyst fails here, the breakthrough will not occur.

Moreover, as I have said, interpretative mistakes can become, by way of implication and consequence, precedents for even greater errors, where the transference pushes the patient in the wrong direction, creating a false sense of self. Each or any of these errors can lead the patient to a mistaken belief of having progressed to a stage of development that has not actually occurred, which can artificially bolster the subject, instilling a false sense of self-value, but these are baseless feelings of worth, destined to crumble in the face of reality. As I have stressed, it is much easier for an abandonic analysand to settle on an oedipal malaise, rather than admit the earlier pre-oedipal fixation with its continuing cathexis to the protective mother and introjection of the frustrating object via systems of prohibition, etc. Here, the patient has a sense of self that is more primitive, less evolved, and in stark contradiction to a state of male or female adulthood. In this case, there is nearly always a certain awareness of the extreme immaturity within, in addition to the state of infantile terror that an analyst can easily miss, with the effect on the subject of augmenting the guilt and shame attached to this neurosis—guilt and shame that bring, after a failed analysis, an accentuation of these profound and repressed conflicts. I have seen this scenario in a series of patients. Below is an example that touches on an incorrect interpretation of the transference.

Example 27: Miss L, aged thirty-two, was the second youngest of eight children. The parents, advancing in years and overworked, had little time for her; the father, however, did exhibit more care than the mother. As a child Miss L was shunted from aunts and uncles to older brothers and sisters, and, as a result, was devoid of affective security. Her clinical diagnosis denoted strong infantilism on a foundation of high anxiety. This insecurity led her to analysis with a male therapist, with whom she immediately bonded. But interpretative mistakes led the analysis in a wrong direction. These errors centred on various parts of the patient's life. The relationship to her father, for example, was interpreted as an oedipal fixation, where, in fact, it had greater primacy as a maternal attachment, taken in compensation for the mother's neglect. Consequently, the analyst also interpreted the patient's bonding with him as an oedipal attachment. This double error was compounded by an insistence that she express her feelings of love and desire, with the anxious silences that resulted being further interpreted as proof of the guilt she felt as a result of these sexual desires.

Finally, the analysand, weighed down by feelings of anger at being misunderstood, terminated treatment. I recommenced analysis with her some months later. It took more than a year to reveal the bulk of material that was essentially abandonic: nostalgia for both the mother and "maternalised" father, primary anxiety, homosexual attachments, the need for fusion with another being, fear of relationships, the repulsion of men, etc. However, her profound attitudes did modify during this time, allowing her to see men as men. She would also stress that the "honour" conferred by the first analyst was his belief that she was capable of behaving as a woman towards him, so she had accepted the assertion, which strongly accentuated resistance of seeing and accepting herself as the child she really was. "You take me back to kindergarten", she complained in our first sessions, but then gradually, with relief, she began to express the sentiment, "finally the truth". Recognising the considerable interpretative errors made by the first analyst, she wanted me to help her acquire security, but had vehemently opposed speaking to me of her childhood under the pretext that, since the first analysis, she was no longer a child.

The more intelligent the abandonic, the greater the danger of analytic failure, where the patient, analytically confident, assimilates classical theories and interpretations, working and using them as unassailable rationalisations for affective conflicts. Assuming a strong authoritative stance "conferred" by the analysis, the abandonic can become utterly convinced that in dealing with these conflicts, it is solely sufficient to exercise reason.

However, this "honour", to borrow Miss L's term, constitutes an erroneous judgement by the analyst and can generate anxiety, or, at the very least, reinstate feelings of discontent and the non-valued self. Having been overestimated in terms of an ability to recover, the analysand comes to feel incapable of satisfying the high expectations of first the analyst, then those who know the subject. I recall the example of a young woman, strongly abandonic, in whom the central abandonment anxiety had not been touched despite having been the subject of a very thorough analysis, in which termination of the final session ended with the analyst repeating to her on the doorstep, "And remember, you are no longer a child."

This statement landed with the force of a sledgehammer. Subsequently, she wandered aimlessly, unable to return home, having fallen prey to a relapse of the most painful and acute anxiety. From this point on, she was internally divided, more conscious than ever of the prohibited infantilism she was impotent to combat, and living in the disquiet of a malcontented self until the commencement of her second analysis that this time treated the abandonment anxiety as well as all of her infantile needs and fears, which were then disabled and dispelled.

In brief, an abandonic will submit to a classical analysis in which his or her central abandonment anxiety is not eradicated, so the subject is left to struggle with accruing internal conflict that, from that time onwards, is a double-edged dilemma. On the one hand, there is the analysis that created awareness of important problems and pitfalls in terms of instinct, castration, oedipal machinations and the ego, which was strengthened through treatment and remains visionary in these domains, and, on the other, profound level, there is a continued feeling of being buffeted and often overwhelmed by the vagaries of anxiety, mania, and incomprehensible fears that seem more anachronistic than ever, the exterior manifestation of which the ego can only attempt to camouflage.

Here, I return to my point of departure, which is to say, the findings and observations provided in recent years by my patients, which have exposed the inadequacies of classical analytic method, or, rather, a failure of oedipal theory, when practically applied to abandonment neurosis.

Confirmed once more, however, through these observations, is Freud's great discovery regarding the Oedipus complex. As stated above, oedipal phenomena in the abandonic are a sign of healing. More generally, we can say that these phenomena mark the first decisive step out of childhood, away from its insecurities and terrors. Here, their importance is also measured as a means of demarcation which identifies two essential states of human development, two basic stages of affectivity, two different structural types of ego and, therefore, neurosis itself.

NOTES

1. Abandonic signifies the neurotic who envisages everyone and everything, starting with him or herself, from the point of view of an abandonment that has been lived and/or is dreaded. The reason this term
   takes preference is because "abandonee" has the disadvantage of providing what may be a false legitimacy for the subject. In fact, experience
   demonstrates that the psychic repercussions are similar whether an individual has actually been frustrated by the absence of parental attention,
   care, and love, or simply believes this to be the case; also, happily, not all
   those who have been actually abandoned suffer from the neurosis. The
   term abandonic, therefore, referring to those we deal with who show
   symptoms of, but might not have actually experienced, abandonment
   seems a cleaner and more robust definition that awakens the idea of a
   pathology dominated by the dread of abandonment, but not one that
   necessarily produces objective facts consistent with quite such a
   malformed familial and social history.
2. Translator's note: in her description of the second abandonic type, inter-
   estingly, Guex does not separate them in terms of being identifiable as
   either pre-oedipal or principally post-oedipal neurotics, as she does in the
   case of the first type. It is not entirely clear if we must conclude for
   ourselves that there is, therefore, no such classification to be made, and
   that the second type, who is described as acutely infantile, only ever
   demonstrates exclusively pre-oedipal characteristics.

3. Translator's note: the phrase Guex uses is *à angoisse proprement dite*, which might understate the case to some, given that, at its worst, this level of anxiety—or anguish, depending on preferred translation, a further complication being that the word is also used to describe the everyday concerns of people considered to enjoy good psychic health—can constantly verge on, and regularly fall into, panic. Guex provides a more graphic description of abandonment anxiety in Chapter Two: "Anxiety, its nature and form" (p. 60).

4. Translator's note: Guex uses the French word "oblative", which, roughly translated, means: reciprocal offering of love. "Oblative" does exist in English; however, its meaning retains the religious derivation of: a devout offering to a deity, which is why the term "reciprocal love" was chosen instead.

5. Let us clarify here use of the terms "fusion" and "absorption" employed by the analysand. For her, as with any abandonic, non-solitude does not mean the type of affective relationship adults ordinarily know and participate in, but, rather, a regression to the ineffable state of union with the mother.

6. The abandonic, whose affective realm of thinking is so coloured by the magicalm is, not surprisingly, also prone to superstition.

7. That is to say when the child becomes obsessed with watching passing vehicles.

8. The rejection of responsibility is the general rule. However, there are cases where, to combat anxiety, the inverse mechanism is deployed, in which case there is always a readiness to embrace responsibility and accept blame. Here, the reasoning is: "If I am at fault, I can always take more care in future to avoid failure, whereas, if it is the fault of others, I remain impotent and at the mercy of their shortcomings and mistakes."

9. Volumes could be written about the relationships between mistresses of the house and their maids. Because she is charged with caring not just for the household, but the mistress herself, the maid, even though she is younger, becomes coated with the maternal attributes of protection on the one hand, and authority on the other. Also, many a mistress of the house fears incurring the wrath of her maid, while unconsciously requiring that they go far above and beyond what are considered normal material duties. At least, in this instance, part of the maid's importance is that she became a symbol of care and love.

10. Cf. Example 1, p. 6.

11. Mrs F is a good example of the positive-attractive, elementary type of abandonic. Although the characteristic psychic structure of the corresponding negative-repulsive, with its absence of interior organisation,

feeble ego, and primitive instinctual life, is identical, the external manifestations regarding the need for love and security are diametrically
opposed. The bio-affective regulatory system in the latter deploys negative and aggressive strategies to ensure that every outcome results in loss.
The elementary negative-repulsive, especially children and adolescents,
are demanding, insolent, self-centred, and conspire to make all immediate
relations totally toxic. This seemingly antisocial behaviour attracts much
grief and serves to tighten the vicious circle of their neurosis. Given the
primitive stage of development, magical thought is of prime importance.

12. Odier communicated his hypothesis to me. According to his observations, what I call prohibitive systems are linked to the frustrating object.

13. In the case of Mr T, there are many memories even from early childhood
where he oscillated between his own critical reasoning and identifications
with more or less absurd judgements made by his mother, but, as a result
of complete submission, he would without fail find in favour of his
mother's absurdities.

14. Freud, in keeping with his affinity for biological perspective, consistently
advanced evidence that characterised oedipal machinations as sexual. In
his wake, there has been too little emphasis, in my view, on the psychological and genetic aspects of the Oedipus onset, with particular regard
to necessary emotional and intellectual conditions that it can produce,
while simultaneously generating an all new psychological attitude to the
exterior world, marking an important developmental step in the child's
psychic growth as a whole.

15. A striking general fact is the extraordinary indifference of an abandonic
boy to his father, with the exception of a father who does not participate
in the abandonment. But in this situation of a frustrating mother and a
loving father, passive masochistic fixation to the mother seems to prevent
the boy being interested in what emanates from his father.

16. Behn-Eschenburg's paper is in English. Verbatim this quote reads: "the
less sign there is of the Oedipus complex, the earlier may it be assumed
to have occurred." Guex's French version, the one I have used in translation, is a little more elaborate: "Moins l'analysis recueille de signes d'un
complexe d'oedipe, plus tôt ce complex a joué son role dans la névrose."
The meaning appears clearer because it provides more context for the
reader who is unacquainted with the remainder of Behn-Eschenburg's
paper.

17. Translator's note: the implication here seems be that psychic maturation
might be linked to biological development, but that it is possible the two
can become separated when the former has been traumatised in childhood and subsequently retarded. However, when the causes of that

trauma have been neutralised through analytic treatment, it might be the case that the psychic developmental process resumes, then naturally follows its evolutionary pathway and, ultimately, reaches maturation alongside its biological counterpart.

18. Translator's note: it becomes apparent later in the chapter that Guex is referring here to *trauma* that is the result of a literal, or actual, abandonment, as evident in Example 19.

19. This can in some children, during periods of affective deprivation, also become manifest in actual gluttony.

    On this point and many others, domestic case studies of young children collated by Dorothy Burlingham and Anna Freud during the Second World War are of great interest. Many of these children, whose family lives were shattered by the conflict, often having been evacuated on numerous occasions, presented all the symptoms of abandonment neurosis: anxiety, clinging to carers, renewed terror of loss, etc. The observations on nutrition noted that eating disorders were less frequent within institutions than the family home. However, where they did appear, greed and gluttony were the predominant symptoms, as opposed to inhibition and the refusal of food (Burlingham & Freud, 1947, pp. 18 & 60, example 3).

20. In his essay on narcissism, Freud (1914c) described two basic types of affective relationship: *der Anlehnungs typus und der Schützender typus*. Abandonment neurosis is a subdivision mostly aligned with the first type, but with a characteristic morbidity, and a dependence on others, particularly for protection.

21. Translator's note: it is not entirely clear why Guex sees this falsely perceived cause of autonomic disorders as beneficial, because she does not say. Perhaps, by way of inference, she is suggesting that psychoanalysis is able to provide a cure where conventional medicine cannot. Which is to say, in the course of liberating the patient from the psychological symptoms of abandonment neurosis, the treatment might also go some way, at least, towards relieving the various physiological symptoms that are suffered as well.

22. Burlingham and Freud explained,

    The developed intelligence of children of over three years old makes them capable of acquiring a certain understanding of actual situations, for example, the real reasons for their evacuation; towards the age of five, this psychical understanding has already begun to act as an aid to *reduce shock*. (1942, p. 55, my italics)

23. During the Montreux conference of July 1946, in the psychiatric forum, Odier highlighted the importance of curative method when treating certain anxiety neuroses, emphasising that sometimes all psychotherapy and, in particular, all analytic work becomes impossible without a preliminary awakening or reinforcing of the ego.

24. Translator's note: from the French ecphorie, a word that seems under-utilised in English, and particularly in psychoanalysis given its utility of meaning: to awaken from the unconscious, as a result of carefully and strategically placed interpretations offered by the analyst, memories previously unavailable to the analysand.

25. I have already stressed how important, it seems to me, it is in cases of abandonment neurosis, where the nature of therapy itself might well be for the analysand the first experience in his or her life of being treated with respect, interest, equality, and stability. See Chapter Three, pp. 58–59.

26. The incidence of gift giving seems to occur with greater frequency in the case of female analysts than males.

27. Here, I am not only referring to abandonment neurosis. Application of classical technique with great emphasis on the impersonal is, I stress, indispensable in the treatment of neuroses, from a starting point that is essentially unconscious.

28. The abandonic's tendency to overestimate and overvalue the analyst must be continually analysed, on the other hand, throughout the course of treatment.

29. A word I use in some analyses to denote abandonment neurosis.

30. Translator's note: the only reference Guex provides for the comments by Mrs Lampl-De Groot and the quote that follows them is in this text's References section, which has been updated to provide page numbers that were not in the original text (Lampl-De Groot (1975).

REFERENCES

Balint, M. (1969). *The Basic Fault: Therapeutic Aspects of Regression.* New York: Brunner/Mazel, 1979.

Behn-Eschenburg, H. (1935). The antecedents of the Oedipus complex. *International Journal of Psychoanalysis, XVI*(2): 184.

Burlingham, D., & Freud, A. (1942). *Young Children In Wartime.* London: George Allen & Unwin.

Burlingham, D., & Freud, A. (1947). *Infants Without Families.* London: George Allen & Unwin.

Fanon, F. (1952). *Black Skin, White Masks,* R. Philcox (Trans.). New York: Grove Press, 2008.

Fenichel, O. (1945). *The Psychoanalytic Theory of Neurosis.* New York: W. W. Norton.

Freud, S. (1914c). On narcissism: an introduction. *S.E., 14:* 73–101. London: Hogarth.

Harris, A. (2015). "Language is there to bewilder itself and others": the clinical and theoretical contributions of Sabina Spielrein. Plenary address to the National Meeting of the American Psychoanalytic Association, New York.

Lampl-De Groot, J. (1975)[1946]. The pre-oedipal phase. *Psychoanalytic Study of the Child, 2:* 75–83.

Laplanche, J., & Pontalis, J.-B. (1967). *The Language of Psycho-Analysis*, D. Nicholson-Smith (Trans.). New York: Norton, 1973.

Odier, C. (1956). *Anxiety and Magic Thinking*, M. Schoelly & M. Sherfey (Trans.). New York: International Universities Press.

Rudnytsky, P. L. (2013). Reading Roth psychobiographically: an interview. In: J. Statlander-Slote (Ed.), *Philip Roth—The Continuing Presence: New Essays on Psychological Themes* (pp. 137–155). Newark: Northeast.

Valéry, P. (1924). *Variété 1*. Paris: Gallimard.

Winnicott, D. W. (1969). The use of an object and relating through identifications. In: *Playing and Reality* (pp. 86–94). London: Tavistock, 1984.

INDEX

affect(ive), 9, 18, 20, 29–30, 32, 41,
    43–44, 57, 62–63, 66–67, 75,
    83, 86–87, 91–92, 103, 107
    see also: unconscious(ness)
  abandonic, 55
  adaptation, 104
  aspect, 64
  attitude, 53, 77
  bio-, 5, 40–42, 46–47, 57, 111
    see also: regulation
  condition, 3–4
  conflict, 106
  confusion, 97
  deprivation, 71, 112
  development(al), 42, 104
  domain, 20
  endowment, 73
  eruption, 6, 15
  experience, 12
  fear, 64
  hue, 98
  infantilism, 98

insecurity, 16, 34, 72
intensity, 73
involvement, 87
love, 53
manifestations, 59
masochism, 14–15, 18, 30,
    65
material, 89
maturations, 59
mobility, 96
needs, 41
normal, 67
pain, 28
primitive, 99
ravages, 67
reactions, xix, 62, 75
realm, 30, 110
relationships, 9, 24, 28, 33, 67,
    95–96, 110, 112
reverence, 2
risk, 28
satisfaction, 62

security, 12, 18–19, 43, 64, 74, 102,
     105
states, 2
strong, 71
substance, xiv
supple, 77
surroundings, 23
symbiosis, 23
threats, 6
aggression, xxii, 2–3, 5–6, 8–9, 11,
     13–19, 23, 33–34, 63, 81–83,
     102
  abandonic, 10–11
  captive, 88
  character traits, 27
  constitutional, 8
  displacement of, 11, 14
  displays of, 88
  dynamism, 63
  elements, 3
  fronts, 2
  importance of, 16
  qualities, 15
  reaction, 86, 102
  reactive, 8
  retaliatory, 51
  strategies, 111
  support, 16
  symbols of, 89
  tendencies, 100
anxiety (passim)
  abandonic, 25, 34
  abandonment, xxi, 1, 5, 7, 16, 21,
     28, 34, 36, 55–56, 59, 61,
     69–71, 78–79, 85, 90, 98, 102,
     107, 110
  acute, 107
  attacks, 7
  castration, 61
  chronic, 77
  climate of, 77
  consequential, 74
  effects of, 25
  eradication of, 90
  guilt, 61

high, 105
initial, 28
intense, 6
latent, 78
levels of, 3, 89, 110
manifest, 72
morbid, 70
nascent, 61
neuroses, 113
perceptions, 65
predisposition of, 94
primary, 106
profound, 104
psychotic, xx
silence, 106
syndrome of, xix, xxiv
attachment, 1, 7–8, 10, 16, 18, 24,
     27–28, 31, 47, 54–55, 57–58,
     90–92, 102–105
  abandonic, 12
  dependency, 90
  disorder of, xx
  emotional, 9
  fantasy, 100
  homosexual, 106
  interminable, 90
  loving, 92
  masculine, 58, 64
  mechanisms of, 33
  mother, 100–101, 106
  oedipal, 54–55, 106
  physical, 9
  primary, 57
  primitive, 98
  refusal to, 33
  syndrome of, xix, xxiv
  theory, xix
autonomy, 35, 53–54, 72, 76, 95,
     112

Balint, M., xix
behaviour(al), xxiv, 2, 4–5, 11, 31–33,
     40–41, 43, 46, 48, 50–51, 53, 67,
     77, 79, 84, 86, 98–99, 101, 106
  abandonic, 16

anal, 63
analytic, 100
antisocial, 111
characteristics, 18
defensive, 44
disorder, 15
human, 86
inappropriate, 87
instinct(ual), 62
masochism, 14
nefarious, 87
neurotic, 96
oedipal, 49
over-compensation, 19
patterns, 100
radical, 52
security-seeking, 48
sexual, 45
Behn-Eschenburg, H., 57–58, 111
Burlingham, D., 74, 112

clinical examples, 6–10, 13, 21–22, 27,
     32, 34, 36–37, 41, 50, 53, 78, 84,
     93, 99–100, 102–103, 105–107,
     110, 112
conscious(ness), xxi, 2–4, 14, 17,
     22, 48–49, 76, 85, 87, 92–93,
     96, 107 see also:
     unconscious(ness)
  awareness, 3, 21–22, 30, 78
  desire for success, 15
  ego, xxv
  emotional rapacity, 84
  expression, 89
  feelings of hatred, 33
  pre-, 14
  rejection, 10
  trauma(tic), xxiv

depression, 10, 24, 51, 84, 92–93
development(al), 17, 19–20, 33, 35,
     57–59, 63, 69, 73, 83–85, 94, 98,
     101 see also: affect(ive)
  advance, 59
  biological, 111

childhood, 29, 69, 73, 99
considerable, xxv
dramatic, 37
emotional, xxv, 4, 55, 97
growth, 59
human, 95, 107
individual, xix, xxiv, 61
intellectual, xix, 75
libidinal, 97
of abandonment neurosis, xx, 78
of thought, xix
phase, 57, 99
problems, 83
process, 54
psychic, 9, 77, 112
psychology, xix
stage, xxiii–xxiv, 4, 9, 41, 43,
     45–46, 57, 61, 75, 90, 105,
     111
step, 111
thought, 76
ultimate, 48

ego, xix, 4–5, 14, 21, 39, 43–44, 46,
     48–49, 52, 54, 61, 75–76, 79,
     83–84, 90, 92, 96–97, 100, 104,
     107, 111, 113 see also:
     conscious(ness)
  abandoned, 75
  abandonic, 9, 23
  analysis, 83
  -centricity, 12, 17, 67, 83
  developing, 61
  disturbance of, xxiii
  domain, xxv
  enfeebled, 35
  ideal, 48–49
  incomplete, 19
  injury, 30
  non-existent, 43
  parental, 50
  positive–attractive, 65
  primitive, xxv
  problems, 1
  strength of, 56, 88

super-, xxiii–xxv, 3–5, 14, 24, 30,
    40–42, 44, 47–48, 50, 54, 61, 64
    see also: guilt
    active, 51
    support, 85

Fanon, F., xviii
fantasy, 14–16, 29, 33, 35–37, 51–52,
    59, 65–66, 100 see also:
    attachment
    amorous, 100
    homosexual, 56
    primitive, 100
Fenichel, O., xix, 75–76
Freud, A., 74, 112
Freud, S., xix, xxiii–xxvi, 1, 5, 14, 40,
    42, 46, 48, 50, 52, 57, 74, 82, 86,
    94, 102, 107, 111–112

guilt, 14–15, 30, 51, 55, 60, 64, 101,
    105–106 see also: anxiety,
    unconscious(ness)
    expressions of, 89
    feelings of, 63
    parental, 14
    superego, 30

Harris, A., xix

insecurity, x, 18, 21, 53, 60, 72, 77,
    105 see also: affect(ive)
    complex, 4
    emotional, 3, 8, 32
    interior, 16
    physical, 72
    primitive, 25
    profound, 22
    sense of, 2, 19
    state of, 20
instinct(ual), 41, 47, 64, 67, 107
    see also: behaviour(al)
    attitude, 5, 53
    conduits, 46
    death, 81–82
    direction, 57

emotions, 69
energy, 44
evolution, xxiv, 75
force, xxiv
impulses, 69
laws of projection, 20
life, 43, 46, 62, 64, 96, 111
manifestation, 59
mobility, 96
purpose, 58
reactions, xix, 75
requirement, 61
sexual, xxv, 43
intervention, xxiv, 3, 23, 41–42, 58,
    60–61, 69, 84, 95, 97
    analytic, 65, 67, 84
    educational, 64

Klein, M., 58

Lampl-De Groot, J., 99–100, 113
Laplanche, J., xiii, xvii–xviii

masochism, 14–15, 32–33, 36, 50,
    56–57, 65, 72, 81–83, 85 see also:
    affect(ive), behaviour(al),
    transference
    abandonic, 14–15
    emotional, 23
    explosive, 15, 33
    moral, 14
    passive, 56, 111
    primary, 82
    reaction, 56, 88
    secret, 15, 33
    self-destructive, 32
    tenacious, 22

narcissism, 58, 82–83, 89, 101, 112

object (passim)
    actual, xxv
    castrating, 56
    change of, 57–58
    chosen, 103

current, 14
erotic, 42
evil, 25
frustrating, xx, 49, 51, 55, 105, 111
gender, 46
love, 12, 32, 40, 53, 73, 92, 95
masculine, 57
new, 2
of abandonic affection, 43
of oedipal love, 54
of rationalisation, 49
of repression, xxiv
of repulsion, 26
primary, 46, 51, 55
relations, xix, 64, 98
rival, 3, 51
self-same, 51
sexual, 46–47
objective, xxv, 18, 26, 28, 40, 70, 74, 84, 86, 97, 104
causal, 97
disposition, 90
facts, 109
opinion, 31
primary, 91
reasoning, 43
sense of self, 30
sole, 92
view, 49
Odier, C., xix, 8, 14, 21, 25, 35–37, 49, 111, 113
oedipal, xx, xxv, 46–48, 51–52, 56–57, 59, 99 see also: attachment, behaviour(al)
admission, 56
advances, xxv, 53–54
age, 58
bond, 78
characteristics, 59
component, 52
desire, 60, 63–64, 99
fixation, 40–41, 59, 102, 105
function, 46
interpretation, 99

inversion, 54
lack, 52
love, 54
machinations, 107, 111
malaise, 105
material, 52, 58, 98, 101, 103
mother, 100
onset, 52, 55, 57–58
orientation, 98
phase, 52, 56, 59–60
phenomena, 55, 57, 107
post-, 3–4, 109
pre-, xix, xxiv–xxv, 4, 46, 49, 57, 96, 99–101, 105, 109
presence, 52, 56
problem, 54
processes, 49
pseudo-, 98, 101
sense, 57, 102
shift, 58
tendency, xxv, 54
theory, 107
thrust, 53
transformation, 52
triangle, 103
Oedipus complex, xix, xxiv–xxv, 3, 24, 30, 40, 42, 52, 54–58, 97–99, 101, 103, 107, 111

paranoia, 34, 65–66
Pontalis, J.-B., xiii, xvii–xviii

regulation, 41, 46, 57
bio-affective, 5, 40–42, 46–47, 111
repression, xxiv, 3, 14, 33, 39, 59, 63, 85, 100, 105
Rudnytsky, P. L., xviii

sadism, xxv, 3, 13–14, 34, 63
self (passim)
affirmation of the, 33, 35, 52
-assurance, 32
-awareness, 18, 97
-centred, 88, 111
-confidence, 3, 76–77

-critical, 13
-deception, 88
-depreciation, 30–31, 74
-destructive, 16, 82 *see also*:
    masochism
-discovery, xxii
-doubt, 21–22, 29
emotional, 24
-esteem, 13, 75–76
false, xx, 30, 105
fear of, 66
-fulfilling, 24
idea of, 30
images of, 29
-imposed, 23
-indictment, 27
-inflicted, 23, 79
inner, 32
love of, 31
malcontented, 107
non-valued, xxii, 14–15, 17, 19–23,
    25, 30, 32–33, 106
ordered, 93
over-valuation of, 22
-protected, 23
provoked, xxiv
-reproach, 10, 22
-respect, 31–32
-sabotage, 87
-sacrifice, 73
sense of, 29–30, 77, 95, 105
-support, 95
true, 26–28
-underestimation, 31
-value, 4, 6, 15, 19–20, 30–31, 64,
    76, 91, 105
variations of, 31
vision of, 21
-worth, 32, 64, 74, 76
sexual, 15, 41, 47, 103, 111 *see also*:
    behaviour(al), instinct, object
act, 46
activity, 44
bi-, 103
caress, 44

characteristics, 40
desire, 44–45, 64, 106
difference, 54, 59
dysfunction, 99
eroticism, 44
experience, 102
genital orientated, 45
hetero-, 46
homo-, xxi, 46, 56 *see also*:
    attachment
    perversion, 50
life, 44
love, 53
potency, 100
presence, 54
relations, 44
rivalry, 101
stage, 63
synchronicity, 45
sexuality, 64, 100
genital, 101
homo-, xxv
    latent, 103
oral, 44
Spielrein, S., xix
symbol(ic), 25–26, 35, 88–89, 110
castration, 45
reality, 72

transference, 85–89, 91, 99–100,
    105
masochism, 3
mechanisms, 86
positive, 34
trauma(tic), xx–xxi, 9–10, 14, 19,
    52–53, 62, 70, 78–79, 85, 111–112
    see also: conscious(ness)
abandonment, 35, 53, 70, 77, 80
catalytic, 79
circumstances, 56
infantile, 6, 23, 62
initial, 78
neurotic, 78
of frustration, 52
original, 2

past, 84
physical, 73
psychic, 84
repressed, 59
severe, 20

unconscious(ness), xix, xxv, 24, 32,
    35, 48, 63, 73, 83, 92, 98, 100,
    110, 113 *see also*: conscious(ness)
affect(ive), 4
death wish, 7
defence, 4, 51
desire for vengeance, 11

eruptions, xxiv
function, 89
guilt, 54
irresponsibility, 79
motivation, 64
need to fail, 15
psychic life, 39
renewal, 37

Valéry, P., 37
violence, 5, 15–16, 22, 34, 65–66, 82

Winnicott, D. W., xx